William Randolph

Flight of a Lifetime

Around the world in a homebuilt airplane

ISBN: 0615524796
ISBN-13: 9780615524795
Library of Congress Control Number: 2011914197
CreateSpace, North Charleston, SC

Flight of a Lifetime

An adventure-filled, over-27,000-nautical-mile
flight around the world by a seventy-six-year-old
pilot who built the airplane himself

For Shirley, who supported the trip in so many ways.

Contents

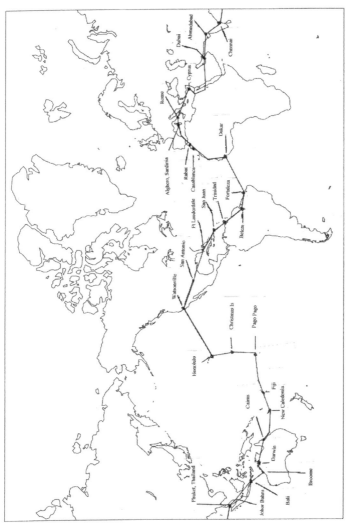

Route around the world

Foreword

Want to have a barrel of fun? Meet new, interesting people? Have a magnificent adventure and live on the edge? Then get yourself a small airplane and fly it around the world. It's not cheap but it doesn't have to be expensive, either. It will teach you. It will thrill you. It will stress you and probably scare you. It will give you great satisfaction. How old do you need to be? Over seventeen and under a hundred. I was seventy-six. I promise you won't be disappointed and you will never forget the experience.

I was determined to fly around the world in a single-engine airplane that I built with my own hands. I thought I just might be the oldest to do it but some older guy beat me to it. I had to settle for oldest pilot of a homebuilt, single-engine, solo flight. I believe I was the fifth to build and fly a plane around the world. My brother-in-law, a retired Air Force colonel, told me I was out of my mind to attempt to fly it over all that water. That didn't deter me because, by his own admission, he would not even fly across the English Channel in a P-51. He had borrowed it in England to fly to France, but turned back upon seeing the great twenty-two-mile expanse of water and hitched a ride on a C-47. He was a four engine bomber pilot.

I read a book by way of preparing for the trip, written by a professional ferry pilot who delivered airplanes all over the world. I learned several helpful things, including that a surprising number of brand-new, factory-built airplanes go down in the ocean on ferry flights. As a matter of fact, two such flights went down in the Pacific during the time I was flying around the world, but I didn't know that then. And of course I didn't know that my life would be on the line, both in the air and on the ground, and that I would be arrested and locked up several times. I didn't know I would have an accident involving an aircraft fire and that jet fighters would scramble to intercept me. All I knew was that others had done it and it was an almost irresistible challenge for me. If I had known about all the "bad" stuff beforehand, I am sure I would have gone anyway.

The trip was about 27,400 nautical miles, or 31,510 statute miles (1.15 statute miles per nautical mile). More than 16,000 nautical miles of the journey was over water—big water. The trip covered thirty countries on six continents, three oceans, eight seas, and four gulfs. Elapsed time was seventy-eight days but more than fifty-five days were spent visiting friends and relatives, waiting for clearances and repairing my airplane. Total flight time was 166 hours. I filed instrument flight plans whenever permitted and logged 79 hours of actual instrument time, about half of which was caused by bureaucratic delays that forced me to fly at night and in frequent bad weather. I was never allowed to complete the departure process one day and leave early the next. Fortunately in a (very) few countries, the process was quick and efficient.

The bureaucracy aside, my trip was a barrel of fun and had lots of color. And by color I mean four arrests on catch-22 deals, three detentions where I was locked up, jet fighters scrambling to intercept me, six legs flown at night against my wishes often in terrible weather, plus an aircraft fire resulting from blown tires. The toughest part of the trip wasn't the flying, although that presented some very real challenges. But they always made me feel invigorated and satisfied that I passed the test. Rather, clearing the bureaucracy in each country was the hard part. After bureaucratic encounters, I felt fatigued and drained. Companies such as Jeppesen that have established relationships with aviation authorities provide flight services that can take out most of the pain associated with dealing with the various bureaucracies. But I built the airplane myself and I wanted to do everything else connected with the trip by myself: route planning; obtaining visas, clearances and permits; weather analysis; flight planning, and ground handling.

The air pioneers like Wiley Post didn't have access to flight-service companies, so I wanted to do it the same way as much as possible. I talked to three others who had flown around the world and all had engaged such companies to arrange their flights at some expense. The companies can arrange for everything on the trip, including covering the "tips" most bureaucrats expect. The cost? One Earthrounder told me he had quit counting after $70,000, another spent over $225,000, and one said his trip cost $178,000. None of that includes the airplane itself. Another pilot had sponsors for almost everything, so his out-of-pocket costs were small. I did everything myself as far as the law allowed, and my trip cost roughly $25,000 and much of that was for fuel. I stayed in good hotels (except one), ate well, and had a more exciting trip than the others, I think. I cannot imagine having more fun than I did, and I saved—depending on the comparison—between $45,000 and $200,000. Even if my do-it-yourself approach caused all the "trouble" I had, I still think my way is better.

As I look back on the flight, I realize that something unusual, dramatic and/or threatening happened on virtually every leg of the trip. I wouldn't have had it any other way. I learned several lessons, which I will enumerate as I tell the story, but the overriding lesson is, just go for it.

Acknowledgements

First I must acknowledge the assistance of my wonderful wife, Shirley, who recorded my daily journal via telephone calls to her at all hours of the day and night(when the telephones worked). She also had to deal with the technical matter of relaying orders for spare parts after an incident in Thailand and chase down answers to questions such as what does one do when brake fluid is unavailable? Until I started writing this I never realized how much work and sleep interruptions I caused her.

I must thank Bob Sliter who took Shirley's emails and recorded the journal on the website of Chapter 119 Experimental Aircraft Association and supported Shirley in fulfilling my requests and comforted her when I didn't call. Bob's posting of the journal on the national website of the Experimental Aircraft Association spread the word about my trip across the country and internationally resulting calls and emails from around the world and more new friends.

Donna Jones, an enterprising reporter for the Santa Cruz Sentinel, took the daily journal and wrote a series of newspaper articles which grabbed the attention of readers in a number of communities around Santa Cruz. Her work garnered the title of "story of the year" in 2005.

Van's Aircraft Inc. of Aurora, Oregon, manufacturer of the kit from which I built my airplane responded in extraordinary fashion when I needed spare parts, even farbricating one to my specifications. Another reason that they are the number one manufacturer of kit airplanes in the world.

Preparing to Build

I was recovering from throat cancer and its debilitating treatment at home in Aptos, California near Monterey when I started my plan to fly around the world. It was one of those "bucket list" things. I had long wanted to build an airplane. In fact, twenty-five years earlier, I had built a special garage providing space to build a Christen Eagle but I never got it done. I had thought for a long time about making a long adventurous flight, but in spite of having owned and flown airplanes for fifty-seven years, I never did that, either. Oh, I had flown across the United States several times, down through the Caribbean, and into Canada, but those flights did not qualify for my definition of adventure because they were not challenging enough.

I concluded that a proper remedy to both failings would be to build an airplane and fly it around the world. I had a plane at the time, a Cessna Cardinal RG, but I didn't think it was the right one and I hadn't built it, anyway. Gathering magazines featuring various airplane designs, I began my search for the "right" one. By my criteria it had to be reasonably fast (over 160 mph cruise speed so the trip wouldn't take forever), tough (able to take the foul weather and rough ground conditions I anticipated), able to lift a lot of weight (extra fuel would be required for ocean crossings), and able to fly fairly high (at least eighteen thousand feet; at some point I wanted to catch the jet stream). I must also be able to build it quickly so that it could fly before my years ran out.

Sorting through a number of designs, I settled on an all-metal aerobatic sport plane offered by the kit manufacturer Van's Aircraft, Inc. It satisfied all my criteria, plus it offered the tandem-seating arrangement of the airplanes in which I learned to fly, WWII-surplus BT13 and AT6, each of which I had owned at one time.

I bought those airplanes soon after I got out of the Navy in 1946 at age seventeen (I lied going in). I was too young in the Navy to do the carousing the others did, so I became a "liberty banker." Two weeks after payday, nearly every sailor was broke. I then loaned money for liberty or shore leave or gambling. The game was called "five for ten for ten," which meant I would loan $5 for about ten days and get a repayment of $10, or 100 percent interest in ten days, a highly profitable and usurious practice. So when I was discharged from the Navy, I had a sufficient bankroll to learn to fly and buy an airplane at six hundred dollars, plus a new Ford that I resold for a profit of three hundred dollars (veterans had priority on the waiting lists at some car dealerships when buying new cars, which were in short supply in 1946).

I ordered an RV-8 plane kit in January 2003 for delivery in six months, except for the empennage (tail) kit, which was available right away. Van's said it should take between fifteen and seventeen hundred hours to build it, so I figured I could get it done in a year.

The main kit arrived around the first of June in 2003 so I reasoned that the first flight should occur around the end of May 2004. Knowing I needed to design and build auxiliary gas tanks, along with their plumbing, and install a special long-range, high-frequency radio system and perform about a hundred hours of test flying, I thought I should be able to depart on my trip sometime in the summer of 2004. When I look back now, the schedule I sought to keep was an obvious pipe dream, but I set my work schedule as eight hours a day, six days a week.

The FAA would require twenty-five hours of flight testing. Being aware that too many brand-new airplanes go down in the oceans on delivery, I decided to add seventy-five hours of flight tests to thoroughly break in the engine and all systems. I also needed extra test time to prove the modifications I planned on making to the airplane, and to establish all the operating data I would need—power settings and speeds for instrument approaches, exact fuel burn rates at selected power settings, loads, and altitudes. I also needed to test the endurance of the seventy-six-year-old pilot.

Then there was the matter of route, flight, and clearance planning. Choosing the route was fairly simple. I decided to break the trip into one-thousand-nautical-mile segments where feasible. That's a distance that can be covered in six or seven hours, depending on power settings. Long enough to make progress but short enough to avoid unnecessary fatigue. Each stop had to have an ILS (instrument landing system with both vertical and horizontal guidance), available fuel—100LL avgas—for my plane, and of course be an international airport.

As it turned out, all of the international airports I chose had one or more ILS approaches. The ILS was important because I could never be sure that the forecasts would be accurate or that the weather would hold up as forecast.

I wanted to avoid long overwater flights because, somewhat like my brother-in-law, I was not too keen on them. That meant a route north to Greenland, Iceland, Scotland; southeasterly across Europe to some friendly Arab country in the Middle East; across India; south to Bali (for a visit); north to the

Philippines, Japan, the Kamchatka Peninsula; continue northerly to provinces of Siberia; across the Bering Strait to Alaska; and southward home. That route would make the longest overwater leg about seven hundred miles, but had the great disadvantage of requiring a Russian landing permit. Having been in Alaska and the North Atlantic in the winter, I knew that I would be comfortable on that crossing only in the summer. In winter, and sometimes in summer, a change of wind can make the ceiling and visibility go to zero in a matter of minutes, and icing conditions can be encountered anytime but especially in winter. That suggests it would be wise to carry enough fuel to get to Reykjavik, find it socked in, and then return to the starting point—say, Goose Bay, Labrador.

The FAA website offers a lot of information on international flights. Through reading, I became aware of a publication called *Ac-u-kwik*. The international edition is a flight information manual—IFIM. The information for this publication is supplied by charter and corporate pilots, I understand. I found it quite complete and an excellent planning tool.

Many countries require permits for overflight or landing. Typically, you need to specify the time of entry plus or minus a few minutes, the date and exact point of entry, as well as things like purpose of flight, operator, passengers, cargo, aircraft type, and national registry. *Ac-u-kwik* lists the authorities, fax, and telephone numbers for obtaining permits, as well as the requirements for each country. However, it does not warrant that any of these people will respond to an individual. Locally written liability insurance is required by a number of countries. *Ac-u-kwik* unfortunately does not help with this nor does the FAA website.

The question of cost naturally arose. I became aware that on a trip such as the one I planned, everything in most places must be paid for in cash—U.S. dollars. I had tried to get an international fuel credit card but was not successful. I had to develop a budget so I would have enough money to get around the world. I had worked in the international division of a major corporation, so I had a good idea of how much it cost for daily living expenses.

Mapping out a route gave me a rough idea of how much flight time there would be and how much fuel would be required. From various sources, I got an inkling of how much fuel would cost in different places. After talking to several Earthrounders, as well as reviewing the Earthrounder website, I estimated the fees I might be charged by various governments. From all that, I formulated a budget—$25,000. I eventually obtained $30,000 in $100 bills and $10,000 in traveler's checks. I had asked the bank for all new bills, but they failed to meet that request. That amount provided, I thought, a reserve for unanticipated expenses, and of course I planned to take credit cards for use in at least some hotels.

My wife, Shirley, had a friend, Jan Hanna, who worked for Jeppesen in international flight services. Jan told Shirley my trip would cost a *fortune*, knowing what Jeppesen charges it's clients who fly internationally. Jan suggested that I get sponsors for my trip, which mildly provoked Shirley to prod me about it. All this came up within a month of my planned departure date.

Building the Airplane

I sold my Cardinal RG and bought a Piper J-3 Cub. The RV-8 is a taildragger, and while I had more than a thousand hours in taildraggers, I had not flown one in about forty years. So I bought the Cub to reacquaint myself with tailwheel airplanes in anticipation of when the RV-8 could fly. It turned out the Cub was unnecessary; I still knew what to do with my feet.

Today airplanes are designed to require very little use of the feet other than for taxiing and certain unusual maneuvers. I understand that when the Navy sends a pilot to the Naval Test Pilot School now, they first put the test pilot—a highly experienced naval aviator—in a tailwheel aircraft with lots of adverse yaw. The pilot has probably never flown such a plane and wouldn't fully know what to do with his feet. Adverse yaw requires you to carefully coordinate rudder and aileron movement in turning, and the nose wheel on modern airplanes relieves you of knowing all the dance steps you might need on the ground in a tailwheel airplane.

I ordered the tools I would need to build the plane. After they came and I felt strong enough for full-time manual work, I started working on the empennage in my hangar at Watsonville airport near my home in Aptos. Van's likes new builders to start there for several reasons. It's a relatively small and low-cost kit, so new builders can get enough experience to find out if they want to go for the whole expensive enchilada. The drawings and builder's manual are excellent. Since I already had experience reading drawings, I found that I didn't need the manual, except occasionally to figure out what I *should* have done before I did something. The empennage was built fairly quickly, about three weeks including my need to learn how to use the tools, plus making the elevator trim tab three times. I would not, however, claim show-quality work. After all, my plane would be for go not show.

Before the rest of the kits came, I spent my time fleshing out the specifics of the route I had outlined. I began to see some of the problems I would encounter. The Russians would require that I take a Russian navigator for traveling over the Kamchatka Peninsula and on up to the Bering Strait. That would entail a considerable amount of money, but the big trouble was I would not have room for him since I had tentatively planned to use the rear cockpit space for an auxiliary gas tank. My IFIM showed no avgas available in Kamchatka or the easternmost provinces of Siberia. The distance from Sapporo, Japan, to Nome would require a still air range of over two thousand miles including reserves, and tank capacity for roughly eighty gallons of extra gas. Eighty gallons plus the tank would weigh over five hundred pounds, and the most reasonable and safe place to put that would be in the rear cockpit. I never did work out an alternate location for all that fuel, not that I spent much time thinking about it. But I knew sooner or later I would have to make some changes in my route because of the requirement for a Russian navigator.

A couple of big boxes containing the engine and the rest of the airplane kits arrived in the first week of June 2003. The time had come for the real work. I had to unpack and take inventory of all the parts and there were a lot of them. Bins had to be set up and labeled—over three hundred in all—to hold parts such as screws, nuts, bolts, washers, rivets, bushings, nut plates, cotter pins, clamps, fittings, etc. There were several sizes for each category of parts and hundreds of items. Without properly organized storage, finding the right part when needed would be a nightmare. I fabricated workbenches as well as cabinets, stands, and cradles to hold completed assemblies. I also built a small enclosed, overspray-proof spray-paint booth for corrosion proofing all aluminum parts.

I did all the work on the plane by myself, except for some pieces I could not rivet and buck alone. Shirley helped me with those parts. I had spent several hours learning to rivet on scrap material, but when my wife started helping, she found it difficult to do the bucking so she wanted to do the riveting. I thought, "Oh, boy, here we go." Using some scrap, I showed her how to rivet, and less than an hour later, she was a better riveter than I. That, like a lot of things, was humbling. There really is something to that Rosie the Riveter bit (Rosie was the heroine of WWII posters when warplanes were built mostly by women). I was proud of her, but I did not tell her until the riveting was all done.

Building an airplane gave me a great sense of accomplishment, and I enjoyed almost every minute of it. Probably the toughest part was installing the engine alone. I don't think it is intended to be a solo endeavor but I finally got it done. There was one thing I could not do at all. When installing the landing gear, it was necessary to put nuts and washers on bolts my fingers could not reach. As I was struggling with them, a young Balinese girl whom we were sponsoring in school pushed me aside. With her small hands and incredibly dexterous fingers, she deftly accomplished in a couple of minutes what I had been struggling with for an hour. So I concluded that in order to build an airplane, you need lots of tools, a wife, and a young Balinese girl.

Although I stuck to my six-days-a-week work schedule, the completion date was moving farther away. I would have made my original first-fly date if I hadn't had to build two airplanes, but that is the nature of the beast. You build a part, drill it, assemble with other parts, disassemble, deburr ragged edges and holes, apply anti-corrosion coating, reassemble, and rivet. It seems you do everything twice and it all burns up a lot of time.

The parts of the airframe that had compound curves—such as the cowl, wingtips, and wheel pants—were made of fiberglass. These came already formed but trimming to exact size and finishing was required. This involved careful measurements, cutting, filling, sanding, more filling and sanding, and then finishing. This was the part of the building process I liked least, in part because I discovered I was allergic to the epoxy resin/fiberglass dust that came from sanding. After a couple hours working, even with goggles and mask, my eyes swelled shut so I had to plan to do this kind of work toward the end of the day.

I decided to leave the fuselage as polished aluminum, but had to paint the fiberglass parts because exposed to UV radiation, they would deteriorate. The airport forbade spray-painting in the hangar because when one of my friends painted his airplane in his hangar, the overspray covered parts of three other planes in adjacent hangars.

It occurred to me that marine paints were formulated to survive a harsh marine environment and boats usually are painted by brush. A visit to a marine-supply store resulted in finding just the tough urethane paints I wanted. When I tried them, I was pleased with how well the paint self-leveled when applied by a soft brush. With some fine-sanding and buffing, the paint looked professionally sprayed on. Well, not quite, but pretty good, and I did it myself without having to buy professional equipment and finding a place to spray. In addition to the fiberglass parts, I painted the interior of the cockpits as well as the instrument panel.

Installation of the instrument panel and avionics was a challenge for me. There were eight electronics boxes and twenty-five instruments sprouting over two hundred wires to run through twenty-five circuit breakers and switches. After consulting a handbook by an old aircraft builder, Tony Bengalis, I learned that it was fairly straightforward if you were careful and proceeded one wire at a time. The trouble with this approach was it resulted in a mess, a jumble of wires. My panel and avionics, however, worked, though I subsequently did have to re-wire it to improve access to everything. While in May and June it seemed the end would never come, I soldiered on, knowing I would miss my must-fly date for my chosen route.

Finally, I called for an FAA airworthiness inspection in mid-August 2004. After a week or so, the inspector and a trainee showed up at my hangar. The inspector assigned the inspection of the aircraft to the trainee and then climbed into the pilot seat. As the trainee went about inspecting the RV-8, the inspector played with the flight controls. He noticed that in moving the stick to the side, one aileron went up more than the other went down, so he called for the trainee to check them out. He told him to measure the travel of each and, lo and behold, the measurements confirmed the inspector's observation.

He told me that I would not be getting an airworthiness certificate because of the irregular and dangerous condition of the ailerons. I tried to explain that it was called differential deflection and designed to be that way to help overcome adverse yaw when turning. The inspector thought I was making that up. I went into more detail to explain the aerodynamics of turning an airplane but he angrily cut me off, saying that another fellow who claimed to be an aeronautical engineer would not listen to him and now that fellow was dead. With that last pronouncement, the inspector left the hangar, calling for the trainee to follow.

I told the story to a friend who is the maintenance manager for an FAA-certified repair station based at Watsonville Municipal Airport. My friend later told the story to an FAA supervisor in the Flight Standard District Office where that inspector worked. Several days later I received a telephone call at home from the original inspector, who said, "If you want an airworthiness certificate then meet me at the airport in five minutes."

After the my earlier episode with him, I set about finding authoritative proof of what I had tried to explain to him. I downloaded the entire chapter on adverse yaw from an aerodynamics book authored by the Northrop Aeronautical Institute.

I took the Northrop material and drove to the airport, arriving in about seven minutes but ahead of the inspector. I planned to review the material with him, and then request a certificate. The inspector soon arrived, accompanied not only by the trainee but also his supervisor. I was tempted to embarrass the hell out of him by confronting him with the adverse yaw pages in front of all present. But I knew that would have a serious impact on the man so after some thought, I chose to show him the papers in private. He apparently had been tutored about the subject because when he saw the papers, he grabbed them, quickly shoved them in his jacket pocket, and proceeded to write out an airworthiness certificate.

Flight Tests

I made the first flight in my new RV-8 on September 3, 2004. The flight went well but I was completely surprised by the sensitivity of the controls. I had been told that the airplane had light, quick controls but when I made the first turn to exit the traffic pattern, I pushed the stick to the right and almost rolled the doggone thing. None of the other fifty or so aircraft I had flown came close to the RV-8 in terms of quick controls. Upon recovery, I continued on for familiarization in the air. I could not have been more pleased with the way the plane flew. I checked out stalls and slow flight, returning after thirty minutes for a landing and ground checks. The expression known among pilots of Van's aircraft as the RV grin must have been plastered on my face as I checked for leaks and other anomalies. Like a little kid, I hurried home to tell Shirley how well it all went, how delighted I was. Happiness is a new puppy or a new RV. Old geezers can still get excited.

The FAA required me to remain within a short distance of the airport for twenty-five hours of flight testing. I used this time to explore all corners of the performance envelope, record performance data I would need for the pilot's operating handbook, program the autopilot and familiarize myself with the high-frequency radio. Several small things required some adjustment, such as re-rigging the aileron controls to correct a tendency for the port wing to drop (some call it a heavy wing). At this point I had no aileron trim installed. Also, a car ran into the rudder and bent it, causing a slight left yaw that was corrected with a small fixed tab.

At this point, October 1, 2004, summer had passed so the northern route was definitely out. I had to replan to avoid the North Atlantic and Alaska and I reset the departure date to January 1, 2005. I needed to nail down the route in order to determine fuel requirement and auxiliary tank sizes. The second route I roughed out was also easterly but largely in the Southern Hemisphere. The route would be Abilene, Texas; Ft. Lauderdale, Florida; Trinidad; Belem and Fortaleza, Brazil; Cape Verde; Rabat, Morocco; Rome; Cyprus; Dubai; Ahmadabad, India; Chittagong, Bangladesh; Bangkok, Thailand; Bali, Indonesia; Darwin and Cairns, Australia; Nouméa, New Caledonia; Fiji; Pago Pago, American Samoa; Christmas Island, Kiribati; Hawaii; home. The route, mostly in the Southern Hemisphere, would be flown in summer weather.

This route showed me that I needed a still air range of about three thousand statute miles (twenty-six hundred nautical miles), including reserves flying at 155 knots (55 percent power) over water and 175 knots (75 percent) over land. That translates into 125 gallons of fuel, or 83 gallons more than the standard tank capacity. I wanted all the fuel to go into the fuselage if possible. Eighty-three gallons weigh 498 pounds, in addition to the weight of the tank and plumbing.

I knew off the top of my head I didn't want over five hundred pounds in the rear cockpit, so I set out to find how much of that weight I could put up front. I measured the odd-shaped forward baggage bay, which was ahead of the cockpit, and then made drawings for a tank. I made a mockup in cardboard and remade it until it would just fit into the bay but still maximize fuel storage. I then revised the drawing to reflect the final dimensions. Calculating the volume, I found it would hold 15 gallons or 90 pounds plus the tank. Then the rear tank had to hold 68 gallons—408 pounds. This wasn't good, but a weight and balance calculation showed that it was barely within the aft limit of the center-of-gravity envelope if I loaded a few more pounds forward of the front cockpit.

I concluded it was doable so I began work on the rear tank, using the same method as on the front tank. With the drawings complete, I prepared to send them out to aluminum fabricators for bids. I sought three bids, but all three companies I approached declined to make the tanks. No reasons were given but I supposed the shapes were too convoluted and the price would have been too high. I wanted the maximum fuel for the spaces available within the CG envelope, and resulting tank shapes had many facets to accommodate my objective.

I decided to make the tanks myself so I ordered the foam boards, fiberglass, and epoxy required. (At the time I did not know how to weld aluminum.) The tanks, like all things being done for the first time, took longer than I estimated to build, but I did it. Installing the tanks was really touch and go as they left virtually no clearance, but with patience and tweaking, it worked. With the tanks completed, it was time for a lot more flight testing. I needed to prove the integrity of both tanks, the plumbing and fuel flow to exhaustion, as well as flight characteristics and rate of fuel consumption at various weights and power settings.

Doing all this made it fairly easy to build up seventy-five additional test-flight hours. In the tests, I filled the airplane not only with maximum fuel load but also weights equaling all the other stuff I intended to carry: tools, spares, survival equipment, rations, oxygen system, personal kit, even the charts, water and snacks.

The first time I took off with maximum load—about 35 percent over the designed gross weight—I was surprised at how quickly the RV-8 got off the ground, about seven to eight hundred feet without conscious control input. The initial climb rate I saw on the vertical speed indicator was eleven hundred feet per minute. I had to push the nose down although the aircraft was not struggling for altitude. I was ready for a long roll on the runway of maybe two thousand feet. I never made any calculations, but in accounts of other pilots with factory-built airplanes loaded for transoceanic flight, takeoff runs were described as "endless"—up to five thousand feet or more—and the pilots worried about runway end obstructions. My takeoff performance was really another plus for the amazing design of the RV-8.

I was quite satisfied with the ability of my airplane to do the job, but one aspect was enough to give me pause. With a total of over five hundred pounds sitting right behind me, about four hundred of which was gasoline, I knew that engine failure or even sufficient loss of power to cause a forced landing would likely have quite colorful and fatal results. A sudden deceleration of, say, twenty Gs would change those five hundred pounds to an impact load of ten thousand pounds on my back. The fuel tank was well secured to the airframe by several stainless steel straps, but I doubt the aluminum structure could sustain such a sudden load without failure. That is simply one of the risks one must accept and I didn't think about it anymore.

I made two long flights lasting ten and twelve hours to test myself and everything else. I am pleased to report we all qualified—barely. The airplane was really squirrelly at maximum takeoff weight, so much so that the autopilot refused to fly it until we burned about ten gallons of fuel (sixty pounds) out of the rear tank. The tanks were positioned so that they fed by gravity to the main fuel selector valve, no additional pumps or fuel transfer required. In flight tests they worked perfectly; simple is always best. In flying a tank to exhaustion, the engine did not sputter or stop. There was enough warning by the loss of power when the tank emptied for me to switch tanks before engine stoppage, which would be comforting at night over a large expanse of water.

I remember one time when I was flying with a friend in my Bonanza. I let my friend fly while I dozed off. A fuel tank ran dry and the engine stopped cold with not a sputter or warning. That brought me wide awake and panicked my friend, who, even though he was a pilot, had no idea where the fuel selector valve was. It was on the floor outboard of my seat so he could not have reached it anyway. So I was quite pleased that the tanks and system I built did not result in a sudden engine stop as soon as fuel was exhausted.

I don't know how many times I flew the loop from Northern California around Arizona and back in the process of testing. But one thing I know for sure: My decision to install the special seat cushions designed for my airplane by Oregon Aero was a winner. My cockpit was so comfortable that I really didn't mind sitting and flying for ten or twelve hours, which for my seventy-six-year-old bottom was a real and happy revelation. On subsequent commercial flights to the Far East, I found that the seats in my RV-8 were far more comfortable than the airline seats in business class.

Planning

With flight testing pretty much done, I turned to the detailed planning I had to do before departure. With my route settled, I began to acquire the visas I would need. I delayed the effective date of each visa as long as possible, knowing by now that timing in this venture was the last thing I could control. I also started to request the permits I would need in Brazil, Cape Verde, Morocco, Egypt, Saudi Arabia, India, Bangladesh, Thailand, and Indonesia. I wasn't so foolish as to think I could line up all those with exact times and dates, but I thought it reasonable to obtain them all and then change the times and dates as necessary along the way. I quickly learned that was naïve thinking.

I sent out faxes to the authorities in all those places and received one reply - from Cape Verde, advising that I would have to forward proof of Cape Verde insurance before a permit could be issued. I knew I also needed insurance for Brazil. My insurance company told me they did not write policies for outside the U.S. and referred me to another company, who told me the same thing but gave me the telephone number for Lloyd's of London. They told me they no longer wrote policies for American aircraft and gave me a number to call in Brazil but nothing for Cape Verde.

I followed up on the Brazil tip and was overwhelmed by the offer of a Brazilian company to write a policy for me at no charge, saying that such a short stay in Brazil wasn't worth billing. I subsequently had to call them to change dates and they were most gracious and accommodating. No one could give me a lead about insurance in Cape Verde so I substituted Dakar, Senegal, knowing they didn't require insurance. I did not want to go to Senegal and that was the reason for selecting Cape Verde in the first place. Lesson learned: If you ain't flexible, you ain't goin'.

Since my RV-8 was experimental—not certified as built by an approved manufacturer—the FAA required that I obtain written permission for my flight over every country on my route. I tried but found no one remotely interested in the subject. So I forgot about it, but I did make sure that I listed the aircraft model on all permit requests and flight plans.

Along the way, Shirley, having been reminded by her Jeppesen friend, Jan, what a fortune my trip was going to cost, began to subtly push me to get some sponsors. Rather than argue that it was too late (it was December and my January 1 departure date was fast approaching). I developed a sales pitch to use in approaching sponsors just to mollify Shirley. I decided to write to the CEOs of five companies, asking not for money but to borrow something I would need for my flight, promising to return the items intact upon completion of the trip. In return I would put their company logo on the side of my plane for the trip, display it at a major West Coast air show, as well as the largest air show in the world, Oshkosh. Remarkably, everyone I wrote to responded quickly and positively

If it was that easy, Shirley said, maybe I should have asked more companies for support. From Aircraft Spruce and Survival Products, I received a TSO'd four-man part 135 life raft (this is FAA technical jargon; the raft was the best-equipped available). Bose sent an active noise-canceling headset to protect what hearing I had left, Mountain High sent a new technology-pulse-demand oxygen system good for fifty-five hours of operation at fifteen thousand feet. And Trutrak Flight Systems sent an altitude-hold module for my autopilot. These things were really needed for the trip and all together would have cost around $7200 to buy. Even if I had to send them all back, they still represented a real savings for me. I should have started earlier and written to more companies. At the end of the trip, I was told to keep the items except for the life raft. In gratitude, all those logos are still on the side of my airplane, and I actively recommend the products involved because they are all excellent.

Weeks passed and the January 1 departure date came and went with me still having only one permit—Morocco. After repeated tries I finally received permits for Brazil and Senegal. By now it was March 1, and I decided that if I was ever going to go, I would just have to wing it and sort it all out on the fly or spend the big bucks for flight-service companies. I decided to wing it. Second lesson learned: Better to ask for forgiveness than for permission. Well, most of the time. One pilot bound for Khartoum encountered a sandstorm and requested permission to divert to Jeddah, Saudi Arabia. Cleared to proceed, he landed and was okay regarding the permit business but lacked a visa. He was jailed until he paid a fine, which happened to be equal to the exact amount of money he had—$1535.

A friend, Ingrid, who is a third grade teacher at the Gault elementary school read to her class a Santa Cruz Sentinel article about my upcoming flight around the world. Her students were quite interested so she decided to have the class follow my trip as a geography lesson. The students had lots of questions so Ingrid suggested they write me letters with their questions, which I received just before leaving. I can't put them all in but here are a few samples:

"Will you take some snacks? You should. Will it take a lot of gas? Do you believe in God?" … Jose

"Will you fly so high that you will need extra oxygen? I hope you have many safe landings" …Giovanni

"I have been in a small plane before, and I cannot imagine going on such a long trip in a small plane. I wish I could come with you" …Jorge

"We were just reading about Amelia Earhart. Are you going to write a book about your experience? I hope you make some new friends along the way." ….Perla

"How are you going to go to the bathroom? Are you going to have any last wishes before you leave?" …Victoria

"How will you make sure you have enough food? I would like to know if you got permission from Iran yet to fly over their land? I will pray for you"……. Liliana

"I can't imagine how you are going to stay awake. Are you worried that something might happen to you? I wish you a wonderful trip and good luck!" …. Fanni

"Are you in good shape? There is a lot of turbulence, you might need muscles to steer the plane. I hope you have a trip of a lifetime." …Cesar

Katie, Ingrid's assistant wrote, "you will be teaching our students geography; hopefully, that fact will give you a smile somewhere along those 26,000 miles?………It did.

Abilene

After revising the dates for Brazil and Senegal, I set March 9 as departure date. With lesson number two, I felt quite free in my preparations and indeed did depart Watsonville, California, at nine a.m. on March 9, 2005. I was finally on my way. The sky was clear and the air velvety smooth for my slow climb to my thirteen-thousand-feet cruising altitude. All was well in my world and it was exhilarating.

My first stop would be Abilene, Texas. I chose it because it was roughly one thousand nautical miles in distance and it was close to the manufacturer of my autopilot. I had originally planned to have just a wing-leveler autopilot, thinking, like Lindbergh, that my not-too-stable airplane would keep me awake on very long flight segments. About two weeks before departure, after all my test flying, I concluded that my autopilot thinking was totally wrong, and Lindbergh didn't have the option for an autopilot anyway. So I installed an altitude-hold module for my autopilot but couldn't get it to work correctly.

I called the manufacturer's customer service, which put me in touch with the president of the company, Jim Younkin. Jim's company, TruTrak Flight Systems, was the most recent sponsor for my trip. The company had also built a special, sophisticated autopilot for Global Flyer, a purpose-built jet that made a world-record, single-engine, nonstop-unrefueled solo flight around the world just ahead of me.

When I told Jim I would be flying from Northern California straight to Ft. Lauderdale, he said, "We're not far out of your way. Stop at our plant in Arkansas and I guarantee that we'll have you on your way with a totally functional autopilot within an hour or so." I thanked him and decided on Abilene as an intermediate stop since it's close to TruTrak.

I was and am completely sold on Jim and his products, but I didn't have to accept his offer because soon after talking to him, I found my own stupid wiring mistake. I called Jim and told him about my mistake, to which he said, "Anyone who had not made such a mistake has never done anything." Incidentally, that autopilot performed flawlessly, and kept me on altitude and on track all the way around the world. It probably even kept me from being shot down by surface-to-air missiles but more on that later.

On my way to Abilene, as I climbed to thirteen thousand feet to cross the Sierra Nevada Mountains, I saw a twin-engine airplane far below. It would turn out to be one of only two airplanes I saw in the air on my entire trip. Granted, I was flying to some out-of-the-way places, but crowded skies that so many talk about?

Abilene was not what one might think of as a vacation destination, but I found a nice town and friendly people. I arrived about four p.m. in good weather, and had plenty of time for a relaxed stay and to prepare my airplane for the next leg.

Ft Lauderdale

I was up early the next day and immediately departed for Ft. Lauderdale in clear weather. I decided to take a direct route, flying over the Gulf of Mexico. It was four hundred miles over water, but since I would later be flying over thousands of miles of water, I thought this was nothing. What it did was test my confidence in overwater flight. There's an old saying that as soon as you get over a large expanse of water, the engine goes to automatic rough, a purely psychological phenomenon. I didn't experience that at all. I guess that was testament to all the psyching up I did on myself, and I never let the airplane know it was over water anyway.

I had talked to Reed Prior of Boston, who flew his Mooney around the world. He flew some very long overwater legs and I questioned him about it. He told me he liked it better than flying over land and asked me if I flew on instruments over the Sierra Nevada Mountains in a single-engine plane. When I said yes, he asked me what I would do if my engine quit under those conditions. I said, "I would just say a mental good-bye to my wife and consign my soul to the Lord." He then said, "Over water you don't have to worry about rocks, trees, or other obstructions, as everything is at sea level. The weather is better out there, there is no traffic, and if you go down, no fire."

I thought about that a lot and prepared as well as I could with survival equipment. My life raft was for four men, it had a cover, desalinization kit, rations, fishing gear, signaling mirror, a flare gun, and dye markers. I had two life vests, waterproof containers for my handheld radio and GPS, and a waterproof emergency locator transmitter. I thought I would be flying at altitudes that would allow me to make a call to air traffic control in the event of emergency.

I modified my RV-8 so that I could jettison my canopy in case of ditching. I believed that upon water impact, the airplane, with its fixed landing gear, would flip, and the canopy, with the sudden deceleration, would crash forward and possibly interfere with my escape from the cockpit. I later talked to a pilot who ditched his RV-8 between Oahu and Maui and the result was exactly as I had anticipated—his opened canopy slammed forward and jammed. Luckily, he had improperly installed his windscreen and it blew out when the airplane flipped, so he got out through that opening.

I placed my life raft unsecured on top of the large rear gas tank behind a bar that supported the back of the pilot's seat. I secured one end of a strong fifteen-foot line to the bar and the other end to the inflation handle of the life raft. With the canopy gone, I reasoned that when the aircraft flipped, it would toss out the life raft and probably inflate it. If not, the line attached would lead me to it for manual inflation. I reasoned that once aboard the covered raft, I would be fairly comfortable waiting for rescue. I never tested the procedure but I thought it was good enough to preclude automatic rough. It made me quite comfortable flying over water, even if deluded.

The first time I flew over seemingly endless water with no sight of land didn't lead to 'automatic rough, but it was for me a very different feeling, different than any I had ever experienced. I felt completely removed from everything, really alone, insignificant. The trip across the gulf and Florida was uneventful and pleasant. On landing at the Ft. Lauderdale Executive Airport, I taxied to a jet center, shut down, and went inside. I asked that my fuel tanks be topped off and inquired about nearby hotels.

The woman present said, "It's spring break. Everything is booked up so you won't find anything and all the hotels are downtown. You'll have to figure it out for yourself and you'll need to rent a car." With that, she threw a phone book my way.

I looked through the book and wrote down the addresses of several hotels, planning to just drive around and maybe get lucky. After writing instructions for access to my tanks, I rented a car from the woman and drove out of the airport. Just across the street from the airport entrance was a hotel called Executive Inn. I stopped, found there were virtually no guests, booked a room, and then went looking for a restaurant, which I found within a quarter mile.

The episode with the jet center and the unnecessary car rental nearly killed my appetite. My little airplane, not being a kerosene burner, perhaps offended the sensibilities of the jet-center folks. And while I am sure they don't give a hoot, I don't recommend them. Unfortunately, I told the story to my wife, who reported all my daily activities to the webmaster of Experimental Aircraft Association (EAA) Chapter 119, who put it on their website as a journal of my trip, and forwarded it to the EAA national website, which is accessed by pilots from all over the world. I don't recall if I mentioned the name of the jet center, but if I did, they acquired a lot of unwanted but earned publicity.

Puerto Rico And Trinidad

The next morning, I filed an instrument flight plan and left Ft. Lauderdale. The weather was good, with lots of puffy little clouds that permitted intermittent glimpses of the beautiful emerald and blue Caribbean, and the white sandy shores of the occasional islands in the Bahamas. I was headed for San Juan, Puerto Rico, which I knew slightly from my corporate days. I stayed in a fairly nondescript hotel that charged me a not-so-nondescript two hundred dollars for the night. This was as easy a stop as any in the U.S. I didn't know it at the time but it was the last of the easy ones.

The following day, I was up early and off to Trinidad. It was quite cloudy and I never saw St. Kitts, Nevis, St. Vincent, or Grenada as I flew over them. A friend who often flew down to the Caribbean told me to go to Tobago and not Trinidad because of the bureaucracy, but my instrument-approach plate was entitled "Trinidad/Tobago" so I figured it was all the same. It was only after I landed at Trinidad did I realize that the pilot was probably expected to make an instrument approach to Trinidad, and, weather permitting, break off the approach and land at Tobago.

I soon found the reason for my friend's advice: It took me three hours to clear customs, immigration, health, etc. Little did I know at the time that three hours in the bureaucratic labyrinth was not at all unusual. The quaint little Bel Air International Airport Hotel, located right on the airport, partly compensated for the hassle. I was up at six o'clock the next morning for breakfast, and off to Aviation Information Services to get the weather for the next leg and do the other necessary things.

I would try to always file an instrument flight plan regardless of the weather because it can and does change over six or ten hours. A flight plan can help keep you out of trouble by transferring some of the navigation responsibility to air traffic control (this would subsequently be proven in Morocco). I had to taxi about a mile across the field to complete my checkout. I cleared immigration, health, and police in only one and a half hours but got stuck in customs.

In addition to my general declaration document, they wanted a "Nil Cargo" form, obviously something proclaiming I was not carrying cargo. The general declaration form told them I had no cargo but that wasn't good enough. I had to file the correct one. But they couldn't find such a form and I certainly didn't have one. After searching for hours, they finally found a used form and then had to search some more for Wite-Out to clean up the form. I dutifully filled in my zeros where it said cargo and signed my name. By the time we got it done, it was very late in the day and I was so frustrated I could kill.

Why the hell didn't I pay more attention to my friend's advice and ask for details? Now I had to debate whether to fly the next leg at night, something I promised myself I would not do on this trip. In the daytime you can see bad weather coming if you're flying in the clear, but at night it can ambush you. After consulting with customs and immigration, I learned they would not let me complete all formalities one day and leave the next.

It all had to be done on the same day. I thought that a couple of bills with Benjamin Franklin's picture would probably solve the problem, but I swore I wouldn't do that either. OK, then, fly at night it was. I rechecked the weather for the route and was assured it would be "a smooth ride, mon."

Belem

I proceeded to take off and made Big Mistake Number One of the trip. A few words about night flight in a small, general-aviation airplane: It can be beautiful and it can be deadly. Flying at night over a city with lights on the ground can be beautiful and fun. Same on moonlit nights. When it's dark and over unlit ground or water, it's the same as flying in clouds—it's instrument flying. The penalty for inattention is spatial disorientation and loss of control and maybe extra work for gravediggers.

The weather poses a special challenge, and if it's truly dark, the dangers lurking in front of you can be a big surprise. Surprises are many times fun, but surprises in flight are usually not good, especially not at night. In the United States and other countries with capable air traffic control systems, ATC can warn of dangers. In most countries outside the U.S. and Europe, there is no effective air traffic control since there is generally no radar. You are all on your own so it's best to know what's out there.

It was dusk as I flew along the coast of Venezuela, a country with a government I disliked intensely for reasons other than Hugo Chavez. Once in my corporate life, I had to fire the manager of our Venezuelan company and I was bringing down a temporary replacement from the States. On the plane, the new manager noticed an attractive woman sitting alone in a nearby seat and decided to go chat with her. I don't know what the chat amounted to but when we landed, she hurried to get off first.

When my new manager and I deplaned, we were immediately detained by police. I demanded the reason and asked to call the American ambassador, whereupon the Venezuelan police decided to release us.

Thereafter, every time I went through Venezuela, the customs people would have me open all my bags and then proceed to examine each very slowly, dumping all my belongings on the floor afterward. Then they'd apologize, laughing all the while. I really don't know what it was all about, but I guess that woman on the plane who eagerly engaged in conversation with my new manager was the wife or fiancée of some high-level official, and she covered her tracks by reporting the encounter. I have since been told that in Venezuela, one does not "chat up" another's special somebody or else risk a penalty of assault, arrest, or worse, and that this is a very old Hispanic mindset.

By the time I reached Guyana, it was dark and beginning to rain. Suriname came next, along with increasingly turbulent weather. I reported in to French Guiana air traffic control, who tried to make me speak French. Fat chance. The controller was a woman whose English was poorer than my French. She wanted a position report on demand about every five minutes, most likely due to lack of radar.

I was on an IFR (instrument flight rules) flight plan and no reporting points were given on my charts, so I had to report latitude and longitude when I checked in. It took a minute or so to look that up, as well as the altitude, speed, wind speed and direction and heading, and write it all down. It turned out to be continuous-position reporting. The controller called about every four minutes, asking for the report in varying English phraseology I could scarcely understand. I repeatedly said, "Did not copy. Say again?" In exasperation, she finally said, "Monsieur, don't you speak English?" I said, "I believe I do. You should try it sometime." That cooked it; I didn't hear from her again, which of course left me time to do such things as fly the plane and navigate.

The rain grew harder, the air more turbulent, and I began to see lighting. That's a bad sign because it means thunderstorm, the nemesis of airplanes. I was in what's called an intertropical convergence zone, a belt in which trade winds collide to create very moist and unstable air, leading to thunderstorms. (Ernest Gann talks about an experience like mine in his book *Fate is the Hunter*.) The lightning spread widely around me and the rain became so heavy, it looked during lightning flashes like I was traveling under water. When the turbulence increased from moderate to severe, I considered turning around to go back to Trinidad, but decided I was already in it so best to punch on through.

As my plane moved through the air, low pressure was created about three-quarters of the way aft on the canopy. This pulled the aft skirts outward, sucking air out and creating low pressure inside the canopy. (This is my theory.) It also pulled water around the S-shaped point of closure, causing it to run in a sheet at the top of the canopy on the inside. As I got soaked, I prayed the water would not get into my instruments and avionics, without which I had no chance of finding Belem.

Thunderstorms are known to tear apart airplanes, large and small, as in the case of an Air France Airbus in 2009, just off the coast of Brazil in this same intertropical zone. One has to avoid overstressing the aircraft. You can do that in part by reducing speed and letting the storm have its way with the airplane while you just keep it right side up. I focused all of my attention on keeping the wings level. I had been in turbulence many times before, but nothing like this.

I allowed the plane to make vertical excursions at will, and while the air currents moved me like a yo-yo up and down one or two thousand feet, I tried to keep the wing leveler but not altitude-hold part of the autopilot engaged. I didn't think the wing leveler was powerful enough in trying to fight the movement caused by the storm to cause a structural problem. The Trutrak autopilot had an electronic gyro that, unlike most mechanical gyros, was non-tumbling, and it always knew which way was up. I thought if I could keep the autopilot engaged, it might help me get through this mess.

Had this been daytime and I could see, I would have disengaged the autopilot. As the turbulence intensified, I lost control of the plane, along with three thousand feet of altitude. At that point I thought that I probably would not survive the night. Even when the lightning flashed, there was no outside reference because of the torrential rain and darkness. The jolts in the turbulence were bone-jarring, and I thanked God that mine was an aerobatic airplane stressed for higher G loadings than an ordinary one. There was no fear, even though I thought I would soon meet my maker. I was very busy trying to read instruments, get the plane right side up, and keep it that way. I did manage to right it, found myself at a much lower altitude, and hoped that the Amazon basin was still far below. I couldn't be sure because I couldn't trust my altimeter due to the low pressure attendant to the storms.

The rain was absolutely torrential, and I could not believe the engine continued to run as it must have been ingesting huge quantities of water. I recalled that World War II fighters, and some modern jets, were equipped with water-injection systems to provide temporary extra power. I wondered if that was occurring in my engine, although I had reduced power to help avoid overstressing the plane. Funny how even in stark circumstances, the mind can entertain such extraneous information. It seemed to me that the fight for survival would never end, but it probably lasted only a few minutes. I was wet, maximally alert, and now receiving the ATIS (aircraft terminal information service) at Belem, my destination.

The ATIS gave me a much-needed, current altimeter setting, and I advised the Belem controller that I would make a straight-in approach on the ILS to Runway 06 and handle it on my own. I wanted no interference from air traffic control. My control of the aircraft was tenuous enough without having to respond to things ATC might want me to do. My GPS showed me how to position to intercept the localizer from thirty miles out. They agreed, so I was good to go.

Rain was still extremely heavy and I could see nothing outside the cockpit. But I was out of the worst of the turbulence and could see no lightning ahead. In an ILS approach, you guide the airplane along two radio beams, one horizontal called a localizer, and one vertical called a glide slope. An instrument in the cockpit shows when you are on or off each beam. If you keep the needles centered, the ILS will lead you right down to the ground safely. I can tell you that those two needles had my full and undivided attention but it was still very difficult to keep them centered due to the turbulence.

When my altimeter showed five hundred feet , I could still see nothing outside the cockpit. I suspected this might happen and was ready to reduce my decent rate from five hundred feet per minute to four hundred, with some power at seventy knots and slightly nose up. I knew you can land using the ILS without ever seeing the airport, but had never done it or even thought seriously about it. I just guessed at the best speed, attitude (inclination), and rate of descent.

Holding a steady attitude as best I could, I knew I was on the ground when I felt the plane bounce slightly. I have to admit that I was more than a little relieved. But I still couldn't see outside. I called the tower and asked for help. They sent a truck with strobe lights on top to guide me to the terminal. I'm sure my landing would have been frowned on by the FAA as being too dangerous for my type of aircraft, but if the Brazilian ATC disapproved, I can recall no mention of it. Unfortunately, I had to open the canopy to get out, but what the hell, I was already soaking wet.

In the terminal I met a young Brazilian customs agent who spoke some English. Great, because my Portuguese was non-existent. I remember the agent and his kindness but that is all I remember of Belem until just before departure. As I was writing this, I discovered among my papers a bill from the Hoteis Vila Rica there. The bill shows a long-distance telephone call, but my wife is not sure she remembers it because there were so many calls. At least I now know where I stayed that stormy night in Belem.

I learned a very big lesson in Brazil. NEVER fly at night In the intertropical convergence zone around the Amazon without weather radar and perhaps not even then. Pay whatever bribe is required to avoid it. Any life is worth more than the three or four hundred dollars probably required. I believed all that going in but now I KNOW it.

Fortaleza

My next memory of Belem is passing through the gate into the airport. I don't know where I went that night, what I did, or even how I got back to the airport. Once there, I set about getting my airplane refueled and filing a flight plan to Fortaleza, a city on the southeastern coast of Brazil with an international airport. This was necessary for entering and departing each country. I expected no bureaucratic hassles, as this would be a domestic flight.

The weather was beautiful, and for the first time on my trip, I would be travelling *and* sightseeing. The distance to Fortaleza was short, only about four hundred nautical miles, first over tropical rainforests and then over lush croplands. Not only should I have landed in Tobago instead of Trinidad, I should have flown directly to Fortaleza. It would have been a leg of about seventeen hundred nautical miles, well within the capability of my RV-8, and the trip in daytime would have been a beautiful flight down the beach. The east coast of Brazil was seemingly one very long beautiful beach, as it was with Fortaleza.

Fortaleza is a city of two and a half million people, founded by the Portuguese in 1500. Later the Dutch occupied northeastern Brazil and built Fort Schoonenborch. When the Portuguese reclaimed it in 1654, they renamed it Fortaleza de Nossa Senhora da Assuncao, since shortened, thankfully, to just Fortaleza. As one might imagine, it means "fort." It has grown to be the fifth largest city in Brazil.

I guess I was concentrating too much on my approach for landing to notice what a large city it was. When I landed and parked, I was soon surrounded by local pilots who had never seen a plane quite like mine. When I told them I was on my way around the world, they became even more interested.

One old fellow—though probably twenty years younger than I—in scruffy clothes asked me where I was staying. (I learned much later he was a very wealthy man who wore old clothes and drove an old truck so as not to draw the attention of muggers and bandits.) I gave the name of a place from my flight information manual.

"That's no good," he said. "Stay at my place."

"I don't want to inconvenience you and your family," I told him.

"Not my house. My hotel," he said.

Looking at his clothes, I thought he meant the Brazilian version of Motel 6. Nonetheless, I agreed.

He introduced himself as Demerval Dinitz, and I climbed into his old pickup truck for the ride to his "hotel." He pulled up to a fairly new, very contemporary, well-designed hotel, and said, "This is my hotel, but you are not staying here. You'll stay at my other hotel." Away we went toward the beach, to perhaps the most beautiful hotel I have ever seen.

On reaching the desk, he told the personnel, "Give this man anything he wants."

"Wait a minute, Demerval. I'm not sure I can afford to stay here and I must pay if I do stay."

"Oh, you will pay" he said with a grin as he took his leave.

I checked in and went up to my room. Every inch of the hotel was exquisitely designed. The glass walls in the large dining room rolled back so it was like being out on the beautiful beach below. I cleaned up, went down to a sumptuous dinner in the beautiful open-air dining room, then retired to my room.

As I lay in bed that night, I reflected on the thunderstorm episode over the Amazon. I realized that I was one lucky son of a gun. I would like to think that my superior airmanship saved my life, but as I thought about it, I concluded that while I did make some constructive moves, luck played a major part in my survival.

Just like in 1946, when I had a life-threatening experience as a student pilot on my first solo cross-country flight. Then, too, it was my fault for getting into trouble. I had left Astoria, Oregon, and was crossing the mountains under an overcast sky, headed for Medford. I had trimmed the airplane to fly "hands off," and picked up my chart to look for significant landmarks to use for navigation..

I must have concentrated on the chart longer than I imagined, because when I looked up there was no horizon, no sky—just white. Having never been in the clouds before, it took a few seconds for me to realize what had happened. I knew I should make a 180-degree turn and get out of the clouds. Trouble was, I had no instruments for horizon reference. I had only an altimeter, airspeed indicator, and wet compass. I tried to make as gentle a turn as I could to the left. The engine quickly got louder and the altimeter started unwinding, showing me that I had lost control of the plane. I tried to correct, but the engine only got louder and the altimeter continued to show rapid loss of altitude.

I finally had sense enough to pull back the power as the airspeed was already at the red line, but nothing else I did helped at all. Quite the contrary, it seemed that everything I did made matters worse. I became concerned that the airplane might be damaged or worse, it might lose its wings. I finally gave up and just sat back in the seat. I was certain that I would very soon die. My life didn't flash before my eyes or anything like that. I was angry, mad at myself for being stupid enough to get into this fix, and angry that my mother would have to read about my death in the newspaper.

Finally, I just sat back, quite resigned and at peace about my impending demise. Suddenly there was a flash of green on the windscreen, then white, and then trees. I quickly took the stick and, as gently as I could without hitting the trees below, pulled up. After what seemed like forever, the airplane leveled out over the tops of the trees. I realized that I had spiraled down into a valley with steep mountainsides on each side of the plane. Talk about luck! I followed the valley as it headed down, and I sure as hell had no desire to see inside the clouds again. The valley led me out to the lower lands along the coast, and I returned to the airport and landed.

Getting out, my knees buckled when I jumped down. I slowly got up and just leaned against the plane as I saw my instructor coming toward me. I told him what had happened and he told me I was going to go on my cross country anyway. After going to and returning from the office, he directed me to another aircraft and sent me on my way. Like the events of the night in Belem, I was very lucky that time, too. (Incidentally, I did not bend the airplane as I had feared.)

After breakfast the next day in Fortaleza, I went out to the airport to check on my plane because I thought I had a leak in the forward auxiliary fuel tank. I had checked the fuel in all tanks when I landed and found the front tank low though I had not used that tank. I had to find the leak, which would take some time. Since I was staying in such a great hotel, I decided to stay an extra day. I concluded that the aerobatics over the Amazon had jostled the tank and had slightly opened a drain valve. I safety-wired it closed to avoid a repetition and also tightened the restraints on the tank. I filled the tank and made a test flight with two touch-and-go landings. Later I discovered I was charged eighty dollars each time I touched down. It made me appreciate how lucky we pilots are flying in the U.S.

On departure day, I woke up at four a.m., afraid that the front desk might not give me a wake-up call. And they did not. I couldn't complain about that since everything else at the hotel was so agreeable—great food and a nice collection of wines, of which I had plenty over the two days.

I went down to the front desk to check out. Demerval had said, "Oh, you'll pay," and pay I did. My bill was four figures—$39.09. I have no idea how they arrived at the figure but I was grateful for Demerval's generosity. He had unhesitatingly loaned me his headset since I had broken mine by stepping on the transmit jack when working on the plane. He simply said, "Send it back when you get home." I did that and have remained in touch with him. He had a Cessna 182 at the time of my visit but he subsequently told me via e-mail that he had bought an RV-9. I even flew down to Lakeland, Florida, to see him last year at an air show called Sun-N-Fun. We had a fine re-union.

Having arisen so early, I had to wait awhile for my ride to the airport. Luis Dietchi, a furloughed commercial pilot whom I had met when I first landed, volunteered to be my handler. I welcomed his offer, especially when told that few of the airport officials spoke English. Luis came to the hotel on his motorcycle to pick me up. Those who have been to Brazil know that the driving can get really wild. Try riding on the back of a Brazilian motorcycle. Even as an aerobatic pilot, I found it "stimulating." I am not knocking Luis because we arrived at the airport quickly and intact.

With Luis's help, we breezed right through all the procedures in only two or three hours. I think Brazil was trying to compete with India as having the world's most trying bureaucracy. We rode his motorcycle to the other side of the airport, where my airplane was ready to go. Although he insisted he wanted no compensation for assisting me, I paid him the standard handler rate of three hundred dollars, knowing that he and his family could well use it and he had done more than most handlers do.

I started the engine, called the tower for my clearance, then asked for clearance to taxi for takeoff. I could see no other aircraft movements on the field so I expected a prompt release. The tower said to hold. I did, for what seemed like more than half an hour. I told the controller my engine was overheating just idling and again asked for taxi clearance. He told me to taxi across the field to the terminal and shut down. "Why?" I asked.

"Your flight plan has timed out. You must refile."

"Oh, $#*&!"

I taxied across the field, shut down, went into the terminal, and up to the AIS to refile.

"First you must check with the police," the man in AIS told me.

The policeman on duty asked for my passport; I can handle that word in Portuguese. My passport had been stamped, indicating that I had left the country.

"What are you doing back here?"

I think that's what the policeman asked; I can't be sure. To make a long story short, it took almost the whole day to sort out that mess, partly because I don't speak Portuguese, and partly because it takes an ungodly amount of time anyway. An English-speaking fellow in AIS finally helped.

Dakar

Finally toward midafternoon, I was free to go. I would fly on a VFR (visual flight rules) flight plan, because AIS said I would have to fly at or above twenty-five thousand feet in order to file an instrument flight plan to cross the Atlantic. Why? I don't know. There is no such requirement anywhere else that I know of. My plane can reach twenty-two thousand feet, not twenty-five, but I said, "Fine by me. I just want to get on with it. And anyway, I will be the only one out there below thirty thousand feet."

Off I went into the fading light on my first ocean crossing. It was still daytime when I crossed the beach on my first big water crossing. That same detached, insignificant feeling I first experienced over the Gulf of Mexico returned as I looked out at scattered clouds and endless water, but no automatic rough. I was about to make my first ocean crossing and at night. The darkness didn't bother me, except that ditching is very problematic at any time and especially so at night.

I had carefully checked the weather, looking at their computer myself to be sure of the information I was getting. The information originated in the U.S. The forecast showed light headwinds at five to ten miles per hour. No problem. I calculated the crossing would require only twelve hours flying time and about eighty-five of my one hundred twenty-five gallons of fuel.

It became a very dark night with a high overcast. I was flying at my preferred altitude of eight thousand feet. One is supposed to fly at altitudes according to direction of travel. Flying eastward on a VFR plan, the correct altitude in the U.S. is seventy-five hundred feet. (It varies somewhat by country.) On this night I wasn't particularly concerned about it, because I was certain that I would be the only one out there.

Reflecting on my situation, I was in awe of the circumstances. I was all alone above an ocean that I could not see, in a single-engine airplane I built myself. It seemed surreal. I had never felt so alone, not frightened, but very different. I could not see anything outside the cockpit—no moon, no stars or lights, just inky blackness.

I was relying on a little box called a GPS (global positioning system) to connect me with Earth, my direction of travel, my groundspeed, my real altitude, the wind speed and direction and the distance to my destination. GPS is one of those technologies that's almost magic. Wiley Post might have given an arm—he had no eyes to spare—for these capabilities, and even Amelia Earhart could have found Howland Island. Navigation has become quite simple, if all goes well, and the tough part is the bureaucracy, the reverse of what the air pioneers faced. If that little box were to fail, I had a handheld backup. If the satellite constellation on which GPS is based had failed, I would have been set back a hundred years in technology, just like the pioneers.

The wonder of my circumstances gave way to the practical business of navigating. I had been airborne about five hours and decided to check the wind speed and direction. My GPS told me the wind was just about on my nose as forecast, but had increased to twenty-five knots. That kind of thing was unsettling, to say the least.

I recalculated my fuel requirement and found I needed fifty-five gallons to reach Dakar, with seventy-five gallons still on board. Subtracting unusable fuel, the present conditions would leave me with two and a half hours reserve on reaching Dakar. But what if the wind velocity increased still more? That thought left me with an uneasy feeling. "From now on, I had better recheck the wind every hour," I thought. But I ended up checking about every thirty minutes. The utter darkness, the big ocean, and doubts about fuel weakened my confidence just a tad. The flight over the Atlantic had been wondrous, peaceful, and satisfying until that wind business came up. Now there was no wafting around in thought and fantasies. It was strictly business.

Eventually, the GPS showed that reaching Dakar was in the bank. I called approach control, giving my position and intention of landing using the ILS approach. I chose that method because I brought no surface charts, had no idea what the topography was like, and it was a very black night. The ILS approach keeps one out of trouble—at least out of the rocks.

I switched over to the tower frequency for the approach as directed. It sounded like the same controller I'd been talking to and probably was. I think Dakar did not have radar, in which case it really didn't matter who you were talking to since the pilot handled everything on the approach.

Not being able to see anything on the ground, I adhered strictly to the ILS procedure depicted on my Jeppesen-approach plate, and received no assistance or resistance from the controller. On short final, I could still see nothing on the ground except a few scattered lights and a large black area. I chose to abort and fly a missed approach. (It's a precisely defined procedure designed to keep airplanes out of the weeds and rocks.)

As I circled for another approach, I called the tower and asked, "Don't you folks have runway lights?"

"Oh, you want lights?" the tower responded.

I later learned that you must request lights because they charge four hundred dollars for turning them on. They looked like two long rows of tiki torches. I landed on a very rough runway, enough for me to think my little airplane would be damaged. And this was Senegal's premier airport. I was directed to a spot where I could park. I gathered my personal kit and several other items such as my handheld radio, GPS, and headset, and headed for what I took to be the terminal.

I recently discovered via Google Earth that the terminal to which I was directed that night must have been an old one now used solely for general aviation aircraft. It was decrepit and was essentially one large room, as I recall it. Google Earth shows a large passenger terminal that I never saw.

The "terminal" was full of tall Senegalese people just standing around in small groups talking. I was amazed because it was in the wee hours of the morning, and it appeared there were no other planes but mine on the ramp. I found a closet that advertised money exchange and I needed Senegalese francs for a taxi ride to my hotel. This small space was crowded with three or four people. I handed the fellow a hundred-dollar bill. He reached into a drawer and gave me a roll of bills. I didn't count it because I decided that if it was wrong, I would not make a fuss about it.

I walked out of the terminal onto what looked like a parking lot without cars, but also covered by lots of people. Almost immediately two fellows rushed up, grabbed all the gear I was carrying, and ran toward the opposite end of the terminal. Old geezer that I was, I started to run after them, not knowing that

I could still run. I had not thought about what I would do if I caught them, which I did after they'd stopped.

The larger fellow, in what looked like an old American WWII GI overcoat, said to me, "Taxi, monsieur?"

Huffing and puffing, I thought, "You bastard. If you had said that at the beginning, this old man would not have had to exhaust himself running." I gave the guys some francs and climbed in the beat-up old taxi.

After finally getting the thing started and driving for about five minutes, the driver turned into a compound surrounded by walls about twelve feet high. When my eyes adjusted to the darkness, all I could see were old wrecked cars and garbage. The driver said to me in French, "Get out of the car."

I thought, "This guy, hanging around the airport, must know that pilots passing through carry a lot of cash. This looks like the end of my trip." I reached into my flight suit for my survival knife, opened it, and got out the opposite side of the car.

I waited for him but he did not come. He was jabbering away in French, which was worse than mine, so it took me a while to figure out what he was saying.

"We will take this car," he said, pointing to another old wreck.

I stood my ground, wondering, "Does it make sense to come to a junkyard to get a better car? Why should I trust this guy?" I considered this for a couple of minutes while he insisted, so I reluctantly walked over to the "new" car with my knife still at the ready. He finally got the thing started and we proceeded to town, with the "new" car actually running better than the old one.

On reaching my hotel, a beautiful building on the beach, I was overjoyed to be there—or anywhere. Having forgotten that I exchanged dollars for francs, I reached into my flight suit and gave the driver a hundred-dollar bill. After examining it, he must have been the happiest taxi driver in all of Senegal as that was probably three months' pay.

I was familiar with Sofitel, an upscale French hotel chain, and chose it because I thought the food would be safer than in other hotels (I had an African-food phobia). My greatest fear in making this trip was getting diarrhea halfway out on a ten-hour flight. Hence the concern for safe food, but a futile concern as later events would prove.

This old man was really tired and, having not asked for a wake-up call, slept until noon. Too late to start out that day so I relaxed, enjoying this beautiful hotel on the beach. When I finally checked out, I was startled to learn I was paying $280 per night plus food and taxes. There was no price given in my information manual. Dear sleep.

Upon returning to the airport, I was finally able after some effort to get the fuel truck over to refuel my plane. While the fueling was underway several small boys gathered around the small airplane. They were interested in the plane, asking a number of questions, one of which was were did I come from. When I told them California, USA, they giggled as some covered their mouths, clearly indicating they did not believe me. One boy confidently said such a small airplane could not fly across a big ocean. About that time, two policemen came up, brusquely sent the fuel truck away, and announced that I had to go with them. They entertained no questions at all, so I had no idea what it was all about. They took me to a building I had not noticed before, and up to the second floor. They steered me into a large office, where stood a very big man dressed in a white flowing robe and a little white Muslim hat.

In beautiful English, he introduced himself as the chief of air traffic control for Senegal and said he was angry. He looked like a very dark version of James Earl Jones but without the glasses. He gave me a verbal thrashing for most of an hour. (Good thing it was in English for I couldn't have followed all that in French.) It seemed I had endangered many lives and broken some Senegalese laws.

"How did I do that?" I asked.

To start with, he said, I had flown the Atlantic on a visual flight plan, thus endangering all those people in the ocean. That was illegal in Senegal. Secondly, I had arrived at night, apparently endangering still more people on the ground, as well as being illegal in Senegal. Suddenly, the chief stopped talking, broke into a broad smile, and said, "No problem. Would you like some tea?"

I don't drink tea and I wanted to get on my way, but I concluded it would be real politic to stay and have tea with the man. Actually, I enjoyed the chat and tea and all the rest of the colorful affair, but I had lost two hours. I hate myself for not getting the chief's name and photo, assuming he would have allowed it.

While there was no bureaucracy coming into Senegal, probably because I came illegally at night, there was lots of it going out. I finally was free to get the fuel truck back—no easy task.

.

Rabat And Casablanca

I filed an instrument flight plan to Rabat, Morocco, and took off. On this leg, I wanted to stay right in the middle of the airway, because this was the leg on which three general aviation airplanes were shot down by surface-to-air missiles. My flight information manual said there had been fighting in Mauritania and Western Sahara. (Imagine that—fighting in Africa.) The route went over Senegal, Mauritania, Western Sahara, and Morocco, some of it just offshore. The winds were really blowing and kicked up a towering sandstorm. I climbed rapidly to get on top of it, getting up to sixteen thousand feet. It was probably unnecessary but I couldn't tell exactly where the dust or sand stopped and I wanted none of it in my engine.

After about five hours, my stomach began to cramp, the first symptom of diarrhea for me. After paying over six hundred dollars for a hotel, the food had *not* been safe. Having consulted a tropical medicine specialist before starting, I knew what to do: start eating Imodium A-D. He didn't say how many pills, so I just kept on chewing until the symptoms went away. Good man, that doc. Eventually I arrived at Rabat but was denied permission to land. It was after dark.

Being on an instrument flight plan, I threw the problem into the lap of the air traffic controller. He gave me vectors (headings) for Casablanca, about forty or fifty miles from Rabat, and directed me to land there. I followed his directions exactly, but after landing and shutting down, two uniformed men instructed me to get into their car. They drove me to a building in the terminal complex and escorted me to an office. Three men there were seated at a table and fortunately could speak English. The only Arabic I know was "Allahu Akbar" and I didn't think that would have helped a lot.

It seemed I had committed the most egregious infraction of the law that one can make in an airplane. I had flown over the ancient city, which was strictly forbidden. The city they were worried about was known as Anfa, which was founded by the Romans well before the movie with Humphrey Bogart.

As these gentlemen mulled over my punishment, I pleaded my case. No ancient-city warning was shown on my charts, no one mentioned it when I filed my flight plan, I was on an instrument flight plan, and of course I hadn't planned to go to Casablanca anyway. After leaving Rabat, I had done exactly what the controller told me to do. Still, they said I had indeed flown over the ancient city, an extremely serious violation. I repeatedly made the IFR flight plan argument, and after a very long time, they agreed it had some merit. After all, the ancient city was still there.

Everyone became friendly and even offered to drive me back to my plane to get my gear. Not only that, one of the officials drove me into town to a hotel. My information manual listed a Sheraton so I asked to stop there and thanked my host for his understanding and kindness. The French receptionist told me the room would be two hundred dollars. I asked for something cheaper. He said, in that imperious Parisian manner, "Monsieur, there are no cheap rooooms in zis 'otel."

I wouldn't have stayed there for free, so I walked down the street and found a genuine cheap hotel, hoping there were no little creatures to disturb my sleep. The desk people were not haughty but nice and I saved a hundred and eighty-five dollars. I found a little restaurant nearby, had a pretty good dinner for four dollars—forgetting completely about food safety—then returned to my very plain hotel room and bed.

Early the next morning, I hailed a taxi and went out to the airport, thinking that since I was going to Rabat to get fuel (no avgas in Casablanca) and had already gone through the bureaucratic hassles the night before, this would be a hassle-free domestic flight. I was wrong. The officials in Casablanca treated my departure for the short domestic flight to Rabat like an international departure with the full, time consuming bureaucratic routine even though my stated intent and filed flight plan specified Rabat as my destination. Arriving in Rabat I had my plane refueled by a nice young Arab boy. He told me that he and other Moroccans liked Americans because they are so kind. Take that, *New York Times*. I took his picture and promised to send him a copy. The subsequent theft of my camera prevented me from doing that for which I was very sorry as I liked that helpful young man. I did send him an email apologizing and explaining the situation.

I think the airfield at Rabat had been built by the U.S. Army during World War II. In any case it was operated by the U.S. Air Force for a number of years. My brother-in-law was once base commander there. It was still morning and I looked forward to getting on my way before noon. The checkout was a nightmare. The immigration official found that my passport already had an exit stamp. Casablanca had erroneously stamped my passport even though I told them I was going to Rabat and filed a flight plan accordingly. Just as in Brazil, I was stamped out of the country only to appear back in it. The confusion was solved by a telephone call to Casablanca, and since the Moroccans spoke English, I was on my way after only an extra hour's delay.

Sardinia

From Rabat I was headed for Rome to visit an old friend, and wanted to land at the Ciampino international airport. The Italians rejected that, since I didn't have and couldn't get a slot, or reservation, to land there. I decided I would stop at Sardinia to sort out the problem. So my route from Rabat would be north across the straits of Gibraltar to Alicante, Spain; then east to Alghero, Sardinia. I was looking forward to sightseeing— Gibraltar, Minorca, Majorca, as well as other parts of Spain and the Mediterranean.

The weather in Rabat was very hazy with the ubiquitous desert dust and smog, but when I approached the strait, I plunged into solid clouds. Fortunately, I filed an instrument flight plan as I usually did. I hated it, though, as I was eager to see the sights on this leg. Leaving the Spanish FIR (flight information region), I reported to French air traffic control. The French exercise control over virtually the whole Mediterranean, except for those areas close to the shores of other countries.

They could tell by both my speech and call sign that I was American. The French being French, contrary to ICAO (International Civil Aviation Organization) protocol, seem to delight in trying to make you speak French. Well, they had a tough time with me and had to speak English, albeit testily.

When I arrived at Alghero on the northwestern side of Sardinia, the skies cleared for a beautiful visual approach and landing. As I said, I like flying on instruments, but on a trip to new places, it's more fun to be able to see where you are going. Sardinia was hilly, green, and beautiful from the air. Idyllic, one might say.

The "bureaucracy" in Alghero was almost nothing. I love Italy and the Italians. They were lighthearted, extraordinarily friendly, and helpful in resolving my airport problem in Rome. I was told that since I had cleared customs, etc., in Sardinia, I should plan on landing at Urbe, a small VFR airport in the middle of the greater Rome area. I didn't even know it existed. Since it was VFR only, it didn't show on my charts. It was far better than going into the large airport, Ciampino.

I said ciao to my new Italian friends and took a taxi to my hotel. The very short taxi ride cost eighty euros, about a hundred dollars at the time. Arriving back at the airport the next morning, I found my airplane covered in ice. March is not yet summer in Alghero and the dew must have been really heavy. The plane was sitting in the shade so I moved it into the sun to warm up because I couldn't fly with all that ice on it. No worries; I had to get fuel and oil anyway. There was no hurry as the flight to Rome would be very short.

I had been trying to get aircraft oil since landing in Dakar, but it wasn't available there, in Casablanca, Rabat, or at the Alghero airport. I had ignored the advice experienced global fliers offered at the website Earthrounders to carry some engine oil and brake fluid. Too heavy, I foolishly thought. I now pass on that advice to future Earthrounders, to have it routinely ignored for the same reason.

As I was warming my airplane in the sun, several Italian Air Force pilots came around. They were helicopter search-and-rescue pilots. I told them that my son, John, was an S&R

instructor pilot currently under contract to the Thai and Taiwanese Air Forces. That tightened an already developed sense
of camaraderie. The pilots were keenly interested in my trip.
Many pilots are stirred by the kind of flying adventure I was
undertaking.

In the course of talking about my plane and trip, I told
them I needed oil. No problem for the Italian Air Force. The
senior officer sent a mechanic off to get me some oil—auto
oil - multigrade 15/30 oil rather than the heavier aircraft oil
I normally use The aircraft flown by these Italian pilots were
powered by turbine engines that used types of oil not compat-
ible with reciprocating engines. After adding oil, I shook the
hands of all my new Italian friends and prepared my airplane
for take off. One of the Italian pilots came back to talk more.
His name was Bruno Manca. He wanted a picture of me and the
plane and I wanted his photo also. Bruno asked for an exchange
of email addresses which we did. He said "I know you are a very
special person because only special people undertake what you
are doing". I was flattered and a bit embarrassed by his statement. "All who fly and expecially those like you who save lives
are very special people", I said. "Please, sir, stay in touch with
me by email so that I can know that your trip ends well". You've
got to love a guy like that. I have stayed in touch with Bruno –
there is a special place in my heart for him. With a very warm
feeling for Italians I took off for Rome.

Rome

The weather, particularly as I approached the Italian mainland, was murky, with visibility about a mile or less in haze—very marginal visual flight conditions. The air traffic controller told me as I approached the shore to be sure to fly below one thousand feet. I corrected him, "You mean *above* one thousand feet, don't you?"

"No, sir, I mean *below* one thousand feet."

Rome is hilly, and on this very hazy day, this guy wanted me to do a buzz job on it. Many pilots, including me, delight in low flight, but flying over American cities at below one thousand feet would fetch you a "ticket" from the FAA. I merrily complied with my Italian controller's instructions and flew over Rome's rooftops, seeking Urbe. No doubt the controller's instruction related to staying below the control zones for the two major airports in Rome but it still seemed like I was getting away with something forbidden.

If not for the GPS, I wouldn't have found Urbe in the murk. It was located in a depression, or "bowl," in the hills. Coming down into the bowl for landing, I allowed my airspeed to get too fast, and since the runway is quite short, I had to go around for another and better approach. I landed at the beautiful little airport and telephoned my old friend of fifty years, Bill Barsanti, who roared out to Urbe to pick me up.

It was marvelous to see my wild Italian friend again. Around town in Rome, I found his kamikaze-style driving had not changed, further evidenced by the rumpled fenders on his Alfa convertible. But it fit perfectly in Rome. I spent a week in wild-driving, no-parking-space-available-anywhere Rome. I liked the sidewalk cafes where we had lunches better than the ones in Paris. The food may have been better, too. I know I will have to defend that statement to my French friends. The weather was unarguably better.

While I was in Rome I learned one thing about Italian law that I don't like. If a company looses money, the CEO is brought up on criminal charges on the assumption that he is guilty of gross misfeasance of worse. My friend , Barsanti, became CEO of a struggling televison company. In attempting to turn the company around he wrote off worthless balance sheet assets, leading to a net loss in his first year. As is routine, he had to go to court to defend himself (out of pocket) against criminal charges, a very lengthly and costly process. The company is profitable today.

I would have liked to stay longer, but I had finally obtained a permit to overfly Saudi Arabia and didn't want to risk trying to change the date. Barsanti drove me out to Urbe, where he and I huddled with Italian air traffic controllers in a thoroughly enjoyable circus of planning my next leg to Cyprus. One controller started off the session, abetted by Barsanti, with, "Let us show you how to beat our system." All in jest, but I love the Italian spirit. If only the Italians could direct that spirit into an efficient government, they might establish one lasting longer than a fortnight. Then again, maybe they have done just that and the result is what we have.

Having established an instrument flight plan to "beat the system," we went to refuel my RV-8. For the first time on the trip, I was able to use a credit card to buy fuel. The fees at this stop were small and paid in euros left over from visiting restaurants in Rome. I hugged my old buddy and took off, bound for Cyprus.

Cyprus

I slipped into clouds at eight hundred feet. Damn, I had never been south of Rome and was looking forward to seeing southern Italy, but it was solid instrument conditions, starting low and extending higher than my cruise altitude. As I was leaving Italian airspace at its southern extent, the controller said, "You will be out of radio contact on VHF (very high frequency) at your altitude for about two hundred nautical miles." He gave me the frequency for Athens control and I thanked him for his lighthearted service.

I called Athens but got no response. As I flew on toward Cyprus, I called Athens four or five more times and still no response. I had tuned guard—the international emergency frequency (121.5 MHz)—on my number-two radio, and tried one more time to contact Athens but had no luck so I forgot about it. Seeing clearing skies as I approached the Isle of Rhodes, I turned my attention to sightseeing.

At least I would see the Turkish coast and some of the blue waters of the Mediterranean. I referred to my instrument-approach plate to find the approach control frequency for Cyprus. Just for practice, I flew the ILS into Paphos, Cyprus, even though the weather was clear. I switched over to Paphos tower and was told after landing to taxi to the ramp, shut down, and stay with the plane.

I was immediately surrounded by about five police cars. As I got out onto the wing, I saw the police, about ten of them surrounding the plane with weapons drawn and pointed at me. Cheerily I said, "Hi, guys, what's up?" The frowns on their faces plus the artillery told me this was no time for levity. Then they all started to ask questions at the same time. I shouted, "Stop! You have to speak one at a time or nothing will get done." And what followed would really have been a circus if the Cypriots had not been able to speak English, at least some of them.

"The Greeks said you are a terrorist," one cop said.

"Why did they say that?" I asked.

"Because you did not talk on the radio!"

"I talked on the radio, but the Greeks didn't."

"Did you know the Greeks sent up jet fighter planes to intercept you?"

"No, I didn't see them so apparently they couldn't find me," I said, trying not to appear amused.

Again, I got angry faces in response. A rapid-fire exchange ensued. "Why didn't you file a flight plan?"

"I did file an instrument flight plan, which was approved by Rome and Paris, which controls the whole Mediterranean!"

"Why did you fly over Athens?"

"Because Athens happens to be on the air route I filed."

"Why did you fly that route?"

"Because it's the established air route to Cyprus."

"You are in trouble, and the American ambassador wants to talk to you."

"How in the world does anyone know I am an American if I did not file a flight plan?"

No response.

The police took me into the terminal, sat me in a chair, formed a circle around me, and continued with questions such as those asked outside. Strangely, no one asked to see any of my documents, not the passport, not my pilot license—nothing.

After what seemed like half an hour, the questions stopped and someone said, "We are not Greek, we are Cypriots. It is not our problem!" Everybody started laughing, including me, as I thought the whole thing was ridiculous all along. One of the fellows handed me a beer—I don't know from where—and for the next half hour, we happily made jokes about the efficiency of the Greek Air Force. Someone said, "The Greeks are very excitable and not too competent. A bad combination." This from Cypriots whom most think of as being Greek.

Having not seen any sign of the Greek F-16s, I was skeptical about whether they were actually deployed. I later learned that a reporter from the *Chicago Tribune* had called my wife, Shirley, and asked if she knew what the incident over the Mediterranean was all about. He had my name and probably got my home phone number from my flight plan.

After my return to the States, I learned that our EAA webmaster had received two messages from the Greeks, one of whom claimed to have been the pilot of one of the F-16s. But the other, Kyprianos Biris, whose function was not stated, said the F-16s took off from Crete, intercepted me over Athens, and then followed me all the way to Cyprus. Well, I was flying in the clouds at six thousand feet at one hundred fifty knots. I don't know how they managed to "find" me and if they did, they did not show themselves or call on guard as they were supposed to do when making an intercept. Biris said it was the F-16 pilot's job to avoid being seen. That's strange.

I don't know how they got to Athens from Crete in a split second. I don't know what they might have been hiding behind between the Isle of Rhodes and Cyprus because the weather was clear. I don't think the F-16 carries enough fuel, even with external tanks, to follow along at six thousand feet and one hundred fifty knots—about its stall speed—for seven hours between Athens and Cyprus.

The other e-mail stated, "Hey, man, who are you and why are you flying without talking on radio? I took off scramble from Crete in F-16s weeks ago to intercept you. Do you know that? *Never do this again*. Kazalios Evangelos, 346 Squadron." I now believe the Greek Air Force did scramble fighters, but couldn't find me and sent those messages out of sheer embarrassment. My version of the story got out on the Internet via the EAA within a couple of days after the incident.

I guess the interrogation by the police constituted formal entry clearance, as they called a taxi that took me to a hotel for seventy-five euros, or about ninety-five dollars at the time. I stayed at a nice hotel on the beach, called Shirley, and filled her in on the sparkling events of the day.

Dubai

After an even pricier taxi ride to the airport, I checked out (easy here) and filed an instrument flight plan to Dubai in the United Arab Emirates, with a route over Alexandria, Cairo, Luxor, then east across the Red Sea and Saudi Arabia to Bahrain, then southeast over Qatar to Dubai. The weather was good and I could do some sightseeing. My wife and I once made a trip to the Greek islands and Turkey, and had planned to visit Egypt to see the pyramids and Luxor. But a group of terrorists had machine-gunned and killed nineteen or so tourists at Luxor, according to the press in Istanbul, whereupon my wife suggested we skip Egypt. Agreed.

So now I would make good on that missed visit. Great to see Alexandria but as I moved over the shore, the sky became murky from dust and smog. By the time I was over Giza, I couldn't see the ground from my assigned altitude of nine thousand feet. I guess I'm just not supposed to see those damn pyramids. The air cleared after Luxor, enough to see the beautiful blue waters of the Red Sea.

Below my route on the Egyptian side, I could see wall-to-wall villas on a Red Sea beach. Some Egyptians live very well. The passage across western Saudi Arabia is fascinating, endless dunes with the occasional oasis like in biblical times, complete with date palms and mud houses but no sign of life and no tracks in the sand. Great photo opponunities but I wondered where they got the mud.

The Saudi controllers were competent, courteous, and spoke excellent English. I was surprised by eastern Saudi Arabia. I found great, irrigated circles just like in Kansas and other Midwestern states. I understand that the Saudis get their water by desalinating seawater. Those great circular sprinklers must spew very pricey water.

Paphos to Dubai as routed was about two thousand nautical miles. I couldn't go direct because that would have taken me into or near Israeli airspace, a definite no-no in the Arab world. An aircraft that has flown in Israeli airspace will not be allowed to land in an Arab country, including Dubai. I flew at one hundred fifty knots versus my usual one hundred seventy-five-plus knots overland to minimize fuel burn. At that speed the trip was a bit over thirteen hours. With a nine a.m. takeoff, I would arrive over Dubai after ten p.m.

I had contacted the U.S. Air Force in Iraq via the Internet and asked for permission to fly over Iraq. There was still fighting going on there but the Iraqis no longer had anti-aircraft weapons that could reach high altitudes. The major with whom I communicated said that in order to do that, I would have to fly at or above twenty thousand feet. I told him I could do that, and he indicated that it was okay with the Air Force but he would have to check with the State Department.

He did that, and when he got back to me, he said that State had nixed the idea, probably worried that I might go down in Iraq and create some kind of international incident. I was going to fly from Adana, Turkey, direct to Dubai, a much shorter route than the one I was now flying. I had had trouble with the State Department before. Sometimes I wonder if they are on our side.

When I did arrive in the Emirates, it was very dark. I was assigned number seven in sequence for landing. As I approached

Dubai, I increased my speed to be sure I was close enough to take advantage of my number-seven slot in the sequence. I later learned there were about fifty jet freighters trying to land at that time. One of the two runways was out of service, accounting for some of the congestion.

The English controller—all air traffic controllers in Dubai are English—asked for my airspeed. I told him one hundred eighty knots and he said, "That's good. The approach speed at Dubai is one hundred eighty knots."

"My aircraft's approach speed is normally ninety knots but I can speed it up to one hundred fifty," I told him.

"You are going to fly at one hundred eighty knots, or you are not going to land at Dubai," said the Englishman in a very imperious tone.

"Roger. One hundred eighty it is. Eight delta zulu." (N878DZ is my aircraft registration number and call sign.) I was on an instrument flight plan, and U.S. controllers usually gave an intercept vector to the localizer—a radio beam for lateral guidance in the ILS—several miles out from the airport. That being the case, I thought if I kept my speed at one hundred eighty knots, I would still have enough space to slow down for landing at about sixty-five knots.

The controller kept me at nine thousand feet until I was almost on top of the airport, and then said, "Descend and maintain two thousand." This instruction required me to literally dive from nine to two thousand. I should have taken my time. My airplane is very clean aerodynamically and I built speed rapidly, even though I put my propeller in low pitch to act as the only air brake at my disposal. Had I not had GPS and known my exact position relative to the airport, I probably wouldn't have been in such a hurry to descend so rapidly.

My speed exceeded the red line (maximum design speed) of two hundred knots by the time I reached two thousand feet. In retrospect I should have aimed for a position ten miles out from the airport to be sure I had the distance to slow down, and the descent could have been less like a dive-bomber approach. I have since resolved to practice slam-dunk approaches to find the rational maximum rate at which I can safely descend.

I tried to follow their instructions exactly, not because I was so accommodating. I just found it easy to get into trouble in those parts, and I was probably a bit intimidated by the strange situation and all the yelling and cursing emanating from numerous heavy aircraft in the air trying to land. "Eight delta zulu, turn right two one zero," commanded the controller. That put me on about a ninety-degree intercept angle for the localizer, and only about two miles from the runway instead of the ten to fifteen miles I expected. A normal intercept angle for the localizer is thirty to forty-five degrees. This also placed me well above the glide slope, not a good position to be in so close to the runway.

My speed was still well over two hundred knots as I concentrated on the CDI (course deviation indicator, an instrument that tells you if you are on or off a radio beam). I did not see the needle move. First it was on one side and then the other side of the instrument, meaning that I had flown right through the localizer and probably to an unrecoverable distance. Again, I screwed up. Not only should I have declined those bad instructions, I should have flown the intercept with my GPS as reference Since I was approaching a unfamiliar airport at night I had thought that flying the ILS would help me locate the airport in the sea of ground lights.

The English controller went ballistic. The captains of all those air freighters above had been relentlessly pounding on the controllers to "get me down you, English twit," and using much worse language. The controllers, by my reckoning, were frazzled, intimidated, and maxed out. The controller began screaming and cursing at me, saying, "You have spoiled our procedure. What is your nationality and name? I will have you grounded!" He then told me to go to Pingo and hold until called. Pingo was a designated holding point following a missed approach.

In the U.S., this would never have happened and if it did, I would have told the controller, "Unable, minimum fuel," meaning I couldn't do it, that I was nearing a fuel emergency. I had been in trouble three times already, and, recalling that pilot who spent three weeks in a Saudi jail, I just "rogered" the controller's instruction and set off to find Pingo with the help of my GPS. Holding means flying around in a racetrack fashion. Believe me, after flying for thirteen and three-quarter hours, it was not a lot of fun to then fly around in circles in total darkness over nowhere. I reduced speed to one hundred knots to conserve fuel, not knowing how long before I could land.

About two hours later, I was seriously worried about fuel, and I was about to declare minimum fuel when the controller—a new one—gave me vectors back to the airport for landing. Apparently all of the jet freighters had landed and they now had time for the gringo. He told me to call the tower after landing and gave me a phone number.

I was more than happy to call the supervisor, as I had some things I wanted to tell him. I expressed my dissatisfaction with the totally unprofessional conduct of the controller. The supervisor was also testy and said he would report me to the FAA.

"Be my guest," I said. Later I met a Scot who told me what I should have told the Englishman but I can't print that here.

I chose to stay at the Dubai International Hotel, located at the airport in a large long building with a rounded top. It was convenient, easy to get to, and I was very tired after being up for over twenty-one hours and flying for more than sixteen. I did not fool around; I went straight to bed.

I arose fairly early the next morning after a restful sleep and explored the building. I found it housed the largest duty-free shop I have ever seen, truly a quarter-mile long. There were things like a Lamborghini and a Rolls Royce, along with bottles of hundred-year-old cognac. These Arabs sure lived high.

Remembering I had business, I immediately got on the phone to India. I had tried for months to get a permit without success. I did get someone to answer and explained my predicament, but the fellow denied that my experience could ever have occurred, and furthermore, he could do nothing to help me so good-bye.

Unlike the Indian bureaucrats to come, the Indian hotel staff was most helpful—with faxes, e-mails, and messages. I spent the next several days using all those methods to contact India in quest of a permit, all to no avail. If I had promised some cash for the respondent, I might have succeeded, but I did not want to do that. Of course I could have used the Syrian company Hadid that I used for the Saudi permit.

I met a New Zealand Air Emirates captain, Morris Tull, who was building an RV-8. I didn't know until recently, when I was going through papers preparing to write this, that Morris had earlier been in touch with Shirley via e-mail. Apparently he found out about my trip from the EAA website, and, knowing I was having trouble getting a permit for India, wrote to Shirley, who told him I was on the ground in Dubai. He then looked for my plane on the ramp and left his card on it. He had some suggestions and a name for me to call about the permit. Again, a friendly pilot offering to help, and I was most grateful. In talking to him, I learned that several other Emirates pilots were also building RVs in Dubai.

Since I was required to have a handler, I tasked him with finding some engine oil for me. Unlike in India, the Arab handler actually did what I asked of him. Unfortunately the seller he found required a minimum purchase of five cases of oil. Finally, someone directed me to a flying school, the manager of which agreed to sell me oil by the liter at fifteen dollars per liter, but they wouldn't change the oil. The flying school was run by Indians.

As I became more familiar with Dubai, I learned that virtually all of the real work in Dubai was performed by foreigners. Pilots and mechanics of Emirates Airline were American, Australian, English, and New Zealanders. Ordinary ground jobs were performed by Indians. I failed to make enough inquiries to find out what nationalities did the remainder of the work. The people in charge, of course, were Arabs.

I bought ten liters of oil from the flying school, using six and keeping four in reserve. I messed up the parking ramp in the process of changing the oil in a strong wind. With my India permit in hand, I proceeded to check out and found that all I owed was just over two dollars for a week's parking. Apparently they charged by weight and my plane weighed virtually nothing compared to the regular traffic.

My handler charged four hundred dollars, which I considered a stiff price, but he did help me with transportation, finding oil, and securing the return of several items, including my survival knife, which had been confiscated by security upon my arrival. They had done a very thorough search of me and my bag on entry. Apparently, they wanted nothing on the streets of Dubai that could possibly be a weapon. On departure they didn't seem to care.

I was given a ride in the handler's electric vehicle out to my plane, which was parked about a mile away. I completed the preflight inspection, started the engine, and performed ground checks as I was sure there would be little time for that once I entered the takeoff parade. After contacting clearance delivery and ground control, I waited in a long queue for about twenty-five minutes.

Dubai is incredibly busy. I later learned that they planned to add six more runways, all with simultaneous instrument approaches, making it by far the largest airport I know of. It was a mistake going to Dubai, given the airport traffic. I had chosen it because I understood they welcomed Westerners. They did, but had I done a little more research, I would have discovered how busy the airport was and found smaller, less-busy places that also welcomed Westerners.

Dubai is returning to its ancient status as *the* trade crossroads of the mid-Eastern world, in preparation for the time the oil runs out. The number of new high-rise buildings was incredible. They were building exotic marinas all along the coast, and a peninsula in the shape of a palm tree with provisions for houses on the palm fronds. Every house would be on the waterfront with boat-docking facilities. According to an English language newspaper most of this stuff was intended for Europeans and other Westerners. They were also building an island in the shape of, and detailed like, the Earth. Recently I read in the Wall Street Journal that Dubai was running out of money for a while after ordering nearly a hundred of the super jumbo Airbus 380s for Air Emirates. This should slow down the construction surge.

Ahmedabad

Waiting in the takeoff queue from Dubai, I was afraid my engine would overheat, requiring me to return to parking and start all over. But it worked out. We took off in what seemed like fifteen-second intervals, filling the sky with airplanes bound for destinations on all points of the compass. As a result of so many flying around the airport, I concentrated on looking for traffic and missed seeing Dubai from the air.

I was quickly out over the Gulf of Oman and the anchorage for what looked like a thousand tankers waiting to move up the Persian Gulf to fill up with oil—a truly amazing sight. It made me think of the mischief Iran could do by damaging or sinking some or all those tankers. I was handed off to Iranian air traffic control, flying just off the coast over the Arabian Sea. This part of Iran was totally devoid of color, a desolate place to live and, as far as I could tell, no one *did* live there.

The weather was good, but the sightseeing dulled after the tankers. Still, time seemed to pass quickly and soon I was in touch with Pakistani air traffic control. A female (surprise) Pakistani controller kindly altered my clearance so that I could depart the airway and go directly to my destination, Ahmedabad, India. (Neither Iran nor Pakistan later billed me for "navigation fees," as several other countries did after my return to the U.S.)

The city of Ahmedabad had a very unusual founding. According to legend, Sultan Ahmed Shah saw a hare chasing a dog. Impressed, the sultan decided to locate his capital at that location and named it Ahmedabad, after himself. The city ultimately claimed the title Manchester East due to a booming textile industry and now is the fastest growing city in India.

At least I was smart, I thought, in choosing this lightly used airport. At the time there were no other aircraft operations on the field but me. After landing and parking, I was met by a fellow who announced that he was my handler. "Thank you very much, but I don't need a handler," I informed him.

"Oh, but you do. It is the law in India."

I knew he was right but I had to try.

My new handler followed along behind me as I found customs and then immigration. Three officials sat at a table where I was invited to sit and fill out some forms. There must have been fifty in the stack. It was late afternoon as I began filling out the papers. The first ones were written in Hindi and they had to tell me what and where to write. They kept looking at their watches. It was after five and I had filled out only about three forms when they said, "That's enough," and gathered up all the papers. Third lesson learned: Always plan to arrive at quitting time.

Outside the terminal I found a taxi and went to my hotel, the Taj Residency. When I was in Dubai, I was in telephone contact with Shirley and told her about the difficulty I was having with the permit for India. I also should have told her that I could have easily gotten a permit by paying off somebody, or by using the Syrian agent I had hired to get me a Saudi permit. That would have saved a lot of people scurrying around trying to help me. She asked the webmaster for EAA Chapter 119 for help in getting me an Indian permit. An Indian pilot named Ravi Thakkar who was located in North Carolina called my wife and offered his father's services. His father had lots of government contacts in India and his home was just south of Ahmedabad.

Amazingly, as I checked into the hotel, the desk clerk told me I had a telephone call. "How can that be?" I wondered. No one knew where I decided to stay in Ahmedabad or even that I was in India. I answered the call; it was Ravi's father. At this point, I did not even know about Ravi or EAA's effort to help with the permit. Ravi's father was familiar with Ahmedabad and guessed that I would choose a hotel close to the airport, which is what I did. I thanked him and told him that the problem had been solved.

I was so startled by the phone call that I neglected to ask how he even knew I was in India. It was heartwarming to have yet another couple of complete strangers volunteer assistance for my travel troubles. This gave me a warm feeling about India, despite the grim warnings of my international flight information manual about the bureaucratic horrors of traveling by private airplane there. However, I felt embarrassed by the effort that had been spent on my behalf.

The hotel was relatively new and quite nice, and the staff kind and helpful. I enjoyed my stay. I got up at about seven the next day and took a taxi out to the airport for departure preparations. My self-appointed handler was already there when I arrived, and suggested that the first thing I should do was pay my fees. I told him the first thing I wanted to do was to prepare my airplane. "Since you, by government decree, are my handler, please get air for my tires and also fuel and engine oil." He declined, saying none of that was available.

I walked out to where my plane was parked and noticed a hangar not far away, with FLIGHT ACADEMY on a large sign above the hangar door. I walked over, found the manager, and, having noticed two American-built Cessna 150s parked inside, asked how he obtained his fuel.

"From the fuel truck parked out back," he said.

"Great. Could you spare some fuel for my RV-8?" I told him about my 'round-the- world flight, and that my handler said there was no fuel to be had at the airport.

"Nonsense," he said. "We will sell you fuel."

I also asked for engine oil but he had none to spare. That was okay because I still had my reserve from Dubai. I asked for air for my tires but their compressor was broken.

The manager (I regret that I did not write down his name) asked if I would talk to his student pilots, who were due to arrive shortly, about my plane and trip. How could I refuse? The truck immediately drove over to my plane and I supervised the fueling. As the truck drove away, the students showed up, about fifteen of them all dressed up in crisp uniforms of dark blue trousers and white shirts, complete with epaulets on the shoulders and wings above the breast pocket. They were an enthusiastic and interested lot, and I enjoyed talking with them and answering their many questions. I believe I may have increased their enthusiasm for their training. They proudly posed for a group photograph.

My plane was now as ready as it was going to be. I turned back to my handler and asked where to pay the fees. We went to the tower and up to where the tower controller was located. I paid my four-hundred-dollar landing fee and fifty dollars for parking, but I don't remember what the "navigation charge" was. I told my handler, "Since you are my handler, get me a permit for Chennai." It was located on the southeastern coast of India on the Bay of Bengal.

My original itinerary included Bangladesh as the next stop. I did not want to go to there, and I hadn't gotten a response to my many faxes and e-mails about a permit. But my information manual told me that if a second stop was made in India, duty would be levied on the plane. I decided to try for Chennai and fight the duty.

In response to my request for a Chennai permit, my handler said, "No, no, impossible. It can't be done!" I insisted and he demurred until we became quite noisy. The tower controller, listening to all this banter, picked up the telephone and called someone. He spoke briefly and then handed the phone to me.

"Where do you want to go?" asked the voice on the phone.

"I want to go to Chennai."

"Then go to Chennai. Let me speak to the controller," the voice said.

I handed the phone back to the controller. He listened briefly then wrote a name and number on a piece of paper. He turned to me and said, "If you have any trouble, have them call this number." It was a number in Delhi and the name of the Director General of Civilian Aviation in India.

That controller was indeed well connected, and I was most fortunate to be in his hearing when the Chennai business came up. I shook his hand and thanked him for his much-appreciated help. This little paper just might give me the winning edge if someone tried levying duty on my plane.

My handler handed me a bill for eighteen hundred dollars. "What the hell is this?!" I asked.

"It is a bill for my services as required by law."

"There must be some mistake. And what services, anyway?" I asked to go see the airport manager and he declined to take me. I demanded. He relented. The airport manager told me the bill was correct. I argued. He persisted. Finally, I asked to see the documentation supporting such a charge. He reluctantly fetched a book and opened it. Two rates were listed: twelve hundred dollars for passenger jets, and eight hundred dollars for cargo jets.

There was nothing listed for small private planes like mine. I argued that since there was no rate listed, there must be no charge. Not so easy. We argued for quite a while. I finally concluded that if I did not want to spend the rest of my life in India, I would have to pay something. I tried four hundred dollars, the same as the landing fee. No luck. Five hundred? No. "You cannot charge me more than one of those huge jet freighters! I will pay you eight hundred dollars." Done deal. This was the first time I had been robbed since I was mugged on the streets of San Francisco, only this time it was legal.

Chennai was still in India so departure procedures were no big deal. There were no other airplane operations at the airport anyway. The weather forecast for the route showed overcast skies most of the way. I filed IFR as usual, disappointed that I would not be able to see India as I passed over. I understand that it's a beautiful country seen from the air.

I had spent considerable time the night before devising a route to Chennai. Foreign aircraft are allowed on only certain airways in India, saving most of them for Indian registered craft. The only way to find out what airways are allowed is to study the very small print on the air charts and many of the air routes are one way. It's a matter of trial and error. You look at a chart, find a route you want to take, then look for the small print somewhere on that route reserving it for Indian-registered aircraft, then choose another, probably less direct route until you get it all put together.

Eager to be on my way, I called the tower and asked for permission to start my engine. The response: "Stand by." I finally got permission to start the engine and asked for clearance to taxi for takeoff. Response: "Taxi to the taxiway and hold."

"Why hold?" I asked.

"We are checking for incoming aircraft," the tower said.

"There have been no calls on frequency in fifteen minutes," I told him.

"We have to be very careful. Safety is very important."

"It seems pretty safe now because nobody is flying, moving, or calling. Please let me taxi for takeoff," I implored.

After a while the tower came back with, "November eight seven eight delta zulu, taxi to runway one two."

Chennai

I taxied to the threshold of the runway and performed my before-takeoff checks, then radioed, "Eight delta zulu ready for takeoff."

Amazingly, the tower responded, "Eight delta zulu cleared for takeoff."

I entered the overcast at about one thousand feet and broke out on top at about five thousand. The cloud deck remained until just short of Chennai. It was a very routine trip in good weather above the clouds with nothing to see. I cannot say that cruising above a solid cloud deck for the seven or so hours it took me to get to Chennai on the circuitous Indian air routes was a whole lot of fun.

The approach into Chennai was visual. Chennai, formerly known as Madras, is capital of the Indian state of Tamil and located on the southeastern coast of India on the huge, ocean-like Bay of Bengal. Chennai had a large airport, recently expanded with longer runways and a relatively new terminal complex. It was dark by the time I was directed to park near the old control tower. That left me out in the middle of the field about three hundred yards from the terminal. I asked ground control if I could walk across the ramp to the terminal. He said no and could not help with a solution to the problem.

I noticed an Indian soldier standing outside the tower and asked him for his superior. He took me inside and led me to his sergeant. I explained my predicament and the sergeant said,

"It is not a problem.", He then ordered two soldiers to escort me to the terminal. They did not consult anyone, but no one attempted to stop two soldiers carrying assault rifles. I offered them money and sincere thanks. They accepted my gratitude but refused the money, which I found refreshing.

In the terminal, I found immigration and a new handler. First, they asked for my permit. "I don't have a permit per se but even better, I have this," I said, producing the paper with the director general's name and phone number. My handler and two others looked at the paper with wide eyes and talked among themselves for a while. They then took me to a room where they locked me inside.

After what seemed like an hour, they returned and let me out, happily saying they had solved the problem. They had written a permit themselves, negating the need to disturb the director general. They seemed quite pleased about it. It was night but I don't think they would have called the big boss anyway. I cleared all the other formalities in only two hours and went off to a hotel.

I chose the Radisson SAS from my information manual since it was very close to the airport. The hotel was pleasant and the staff friendly and gracious, as is probably usual for Indian hotels. It was late at night and I was very tired so I decided to stay two nights. The next leg was a long overwater flight, and I had already realized that my manual was not exaggerating about the difficulty of Indian bureaucracy. My wife tells me to relax but dealing with mindless rules is exhausting for me.

I slept in until about eight the next morning. I tried to call my new handler, using his business card for reference, but received endless busy signals. I went down to the desk and mentioned that I couldn't get through on the telephone. The desk clerk told me that everyone was having trouble with the phones. Chennai was in the midst of changing all their central office equipment to expand numbers from five to seven digits. All old numbers were now invalid, no new phone book was yet available, and a call to information yielded only endless busy signals. My "helpful handler" could have mentioned this.

The concierge suggested a solution: Send one of the clerks over to the airport, look up the handler, and get his new phone number. Incredibly, it worked—after two tries. I called the handler and told him I wanted to go out to the airport, refuel my airplane, and get it ready for an early (that word seemed to have no meaning when dealing with private aircraft schedules outside the U.S.) departure the next day (I was ever the optimist). He said, "No, no, come tomorrow and do everything at once."

After some discussion about it, I agreed and told him I would meet him at seven a.m. at the main entrance to the terminal. The total time involved in calling my handler was about four hours. Just go with the flow. Yeah, but that's hard to do.

I planned, to the extent that I could, for my flight the next day and reviewed the requirements for the rest of the journey. I then went down for an early dinner so I could get to bed early. I ordered an Indian red wine in the pleasant restaurant. When it came, I mindlessly asked the waiter how long India had been making wine. He said he didn't know but was sure it was more than four thousand years. Well, I thought, they must be pretty good at it by now. Maybe, but the wine I got was awful. I drank it anyway and went to bed after calling Shirley.

I went to the airport early as planned, but there no handler. He did not arrive at seven as agreed but came sauntering along at eight fifteen. I was not a happy camper. We went first to immigration and a new crowd asked for my departure permit. No worries; I produced the paper with the director general's name and number. "Call that number and you will find everything is good to go," I told them. They just stared at the paper, then mumbled among themselves and locked me in a room just like before.

When they later let me out, they happily declared they had solved the problem...by writing a permit themselves. Now I knew for sure that no one had the courage to call the big chief. My son, a commercial pilot who flies throughout the Far East, later told me that he gathers the names and phone numbers of high-ranking officials. Then, if he hits an unanticipated snag in the bureaucracy, he produces a name and phone number. No one, he assures me, will ever call. Maybe, but he has more chutzpa than I.

The rest of the bureaucratic process dragged on for another three and a half hours, partly because all the places you're required to visit are so scattered. By that time I was so thoroughly frustrated that I just wanted to go back to bed and we hadn't even fueled the plane yet. "Get the fuel truck, and I need air for my tires," I told my handler. He did get the fuel truck but said no air was available. "Maybe you can get air at your next stop." Brilliant.

After some delay, the fuel truck drove up to my plane. The driver got out and said, "We cannot pump gas today."

"Why not?" I demanded.

"Because it is Sunday and we are not allowed to sell gas on Sunday."

"I didn't realize you were such a devout Christian nation," I told him cynically. I grabbed my handler by the lapels, really wanting to throttle him. "You told me to wait until today. Now look at the mess we are in. I want to talk to your boss, whoever that is!"

He said, "Maybe if you write a letter to Delhi absolving us of responsibility, we can fuel your plane."

I exploded. "Write a letter to Delhi! That could take two weeks!"

"No, no," he said, handing me a piece of paper. "Write the letter now and then we can go ahead with the fueling."

What kind of nonsense was this? But I went along with it. I warned the fuel guys, "That fuel has just come from cold tanks and it's about a hundred and thirty degrees out on this tarmac. The fuel will rapidly expand so leave room for it."

"Do not worry, sir. We are professionals."

I told them to fill the aft cockpit tank first, then I proceeded to write the letter to Delhi on the wing of my plane.

Soon the smell of aviation gas wafted my way. I looked up and the tarmac was flooded with gas. When I looked over, the fuel guys were happily talking among themselves, totally ignoring the fueling process. I yelled at them to stop. "Damn it! You have flooded my airplane, my clothes, and all my gear with gas, and it still is going to expand and flood some more."

"We can defuel a bit."

"Are you sure you know how to do that?"

"Oh, yes, we do it all the time."

I watched as they put another ten gallons of avgas through my plane onto the tarmac. I exploded, shouting, "Stop! You must have put fifty gallons of your gas on the tarmac."

"Oh, no sir, it is not our gas, it is your gas."

"*The hell it is!*"

We argued that point for quite a while. At length, I concluded I would be endlessly mired in Indian turmoil if I did not pay the three or four hundred dollars for the tarmac gas. Smiling to myself, I started counting out rupees. The Indians went ballistic. "We cannot accept rupees. You must pay us in U.S. dollars." I pretended to have none. They were beside themselves. Fueled on Sunday and paid in rupees!

I turned to my handler and barked, "Damn it, look at what you caused. It's so late now, I must wait and depart tomorrow."

He looked me straight in the eye and said, "You want to go through all this again tomorrow?" I could have killed him right then and there but the irony was, he was right. I just turned and climbed into my plane.

I am not especially hot-tempered but I do get angry at certain things, especially bureaucratic nonsense. Shirley knows this so before I left home, she had counseled me: "When you go to one of those places, don't talk. Just listen and agree with everything they say." I followed that advice and it worked fairly well—up until India, where I could handle it no longer. I lost it.

I called the tower and asked for permission to start my engine. How free and wonderful it is to fly in the United States. In India you can't even start your engine without express permission. The tower said to stand by. Stand by, indeed. The temperature in my cockpit must have been a hundred and twenty. My canopy was a Plexiglas bubble, and the temperature on Chennai's tarmac was hot enough to fry an egg. Sitting in the cockpit for minutes left me drenched in sweat and really hot under the collar even though the canopy was partly open. Minutes went by before the tower came back with, "November eight seven eight delta zulu, you can start your engine."

I asked for clearance to taxi for takeoff. The tower said, "Taxi to the taxiway and hold."

"Hold?!" I exclaimed. "There is no airplane moving on the field except mine. Why do I have to hold?"

"Because there is an airliner on final," he said.

"I heard him. He's twenty-five miles out. I could be in position to take off before he gets here."

"That doesn't matter. You have to hold and you cannot be on the taxiway while he is landing."

Before I was given clearance for takeoff, I had to call the tower and tell them that my engine was overheating and that I would have to return to the ramp and shut down. I parked in the shadow of the old tower, but it still took a long time for my engine to cool even a little bit.

I eventually got permission to start up again and taxi to the taxiway and hold. It was a short hold this time. The tower called and told me to return to the ramp and shut down. "Why?" I asked.

"Because you now owe more parking fees." Unbelievable!

I did as instructed and went back to pay more fees. The fellow in AIS said, "You do not owe more parking fees. We overcharged you in the beginning. We know how it works around here." I told them, "Of all the people in this airport, you seem to be the only ones who know what you are doing. Please impress upon the tower that I have fully paid all fees. And thanks."

Another trying, sweltering hour passed before I could get back to my plane and get airborne. When I took off, I knew I would be flying into a night harboring very bad weather, but it seemed that anything was better than another day of the infuriating bureaucracy that was India's. Several times I pointed out that the rules made no sense, to which I usually got agreement with the caveat, "The English were here, you know, and they made the rules." I never got a response when I pointed out that the English had been gone for nearly a century.

Phuket

The flight to Phuket, Thailand, is not an especially long leg, only twelve hundred nautical miles, but the forecast showed the weather to be awful, with a line of thunderstorms across my path. I had looked at their computer display, carefully noted the source of the forecast (London), and spent time to study the movement of the storms. I felt the information was reliable and chose to gamble with it.

It was still daylight when I left Chennai and I was quickly out over water again. That strange feeling of detachment and insignificance returned as I lost sight of land. The sky grew darker and the hours droned on. The screen on my Garmin 430 global navigator showed my little airplane moving slowly across the huge Bay of Bengal (better to call it the Bengal Sea or Ocean), then the Andaman Islands and Andaman Sea.

Despite having spent twenty-five years in the computer industry, I still wonder at these marvelous devices. I have heard it said that if technology is advanced enough, it really is magic and it seemed so that night. It was even darker than the Atlantic crossing—total blackness, the blackest black I have ever seen. It was a world of its own, something separate from earthly things, ethereal. It seemed nothing existed beyond me and my little plane. I stumble here because I can't find the words to exactly describe my feelings on that night.

I didn't try turning out all the lights; I tried that over the Atlantic and it didn't help me see anything. The air began to get rougher and soon came the rain. I slowed to a hundred forty knots as I didn't know how turbulent it would get. I thought of going lower to seek less turbulent air, but since I didn't know what the true air pressure was, I couldn't rely on my altimeter for precision. I couldn't see the ocean or anything else.

I hadn't seen lightning yet but knew I was getting close to the line of storms. I waited a bit longer, then turned northeast to skirt the position of the southwesterly-drifting thunderstorms, and hoped the forecast was accurate and that the satellite imagery held up. As I looked back toward my starboard quarter, I saw a ripple of lightning among a line of cells. I reasoned that I would be able to tell, by a reduction of both the rain and turbulence, when I had rounded entent of the storms. Again, I cursed myself for not buying the stormscope, which could have pointed out the location of the worst of the cell activity. That instrument would have made me feel a lot safer and probably shortened the detour I made.

I flew on a northeasterly heading for an hour and then corrected to get back on course. I made it around the line of storms just as I calculated, but the rain continued on the backside and I encountered adverse winds as I crossed the Andaman Sea.

My detour added perhaps three or four hundred miles to the flight. This event proved my theory that regardless of the planned distance, take more than enough gasoline because you never know when you will need it or how much. As the hours dragged on, I realized that I was very, very tired, mostly from fighting with the Indian bureaucrats. Anxiety didn't help, either.

Arriving in Thai airspace, I called Phuket and learned that there were four of us to land—three jetliners and me. Luckily I was number one in the sequence. I flew the ILS, knowing it would be an actual instrument approach in thick clouds and heavy rain. The controller said, "Maintain one hundred and sixty knots on final." My plane lands at about sixty knots and I usually fly final at eighty. But I knew the runway was eleven-thousand-feet long and I deceived myself into thinking I could get slowed down for landing.

It was so easy to get into trouble that I did not want to ignore the controller's instruction, as I would have in the States. (Of course, in the States, the most extreme instruction would be, "Give me your best speed.") I could have eliminated the one-hundred-sixty-knot problem by declining the approach clearance and going to the end of the line. No way. After an exhausting day and flying all night in terrible weather, I just wanted to get on the ground.

I broke out of the clouds at the anticipated two-hundred-foot level. The runway lights, blurred in my rain-dashed windscreen, were right in from of me and I was still going one hundred sixty knots. I chopped the power and began fishtailing as wildly as I could. Fishtailing is rapidly moving the rudder from side to side to make the airplane skid, which creates extra drag. I had put my prop in low pitch, which helps as an air brake, and the only other device I had to create drag was flaps. The maximum flap speed is only ninety knots, no use to me in this case.

It briefly flashed through my mind that I could sure use the speed brakes I had toyed with but never built. I knew I should have flown a missed approach but my fatigue said get it on the ground. I forgot that fatigue can lead to very bad judgment.

I saw the end of the runway coming and didn't know how fast I was going, but I forced the plane onto the ground. Immediately the left tire blew. I was going too fast for it, and it had been low in pressure anyway. Now this condition made the plane want to spin around or ground-loop, which could lead to a big fireball. There was no time to think, just react, and I kicked the right rudder so hard the right tire burst as well. That was good because now I could go straight. Many hours of experience in old, poor-ground-handling taildraggers had served me well. And plain old good luck didn't hurt.

It was still raining heavily and I didn't want to get off the runway for fear of nosing over and damaging my propeller, so I kept moving, but not all that fast on nearly full power and disintegrating wheels. I had to clear the runway for those jets following me. As I neared the end of the runway, flames coming over the leading edge of the wings grabbed my attention. The friction of running on the bare wheel rims had set the remains of the tires on fire, which burned fiercely. I called the tower. "Eight delta zulu has a problem!"

"Yes, sir, we can see it."

"Then please tell the firemen to hurry!"

After clearing the runway, I kicked the plane off the taxiway into the grass, got out with my pitifully small fire extinguisher, and in seconds exhausted it without bothering the fires. I ran back to the cockpit and got my high-altitude jacket and tried to smother one of the tire fires. The jacket went up in flames in an instant. I was trying to think of something else to do because the fires were right under the wing fuel tanks, which still held a lot of gas.

Before I could think of anything, two Oshkosh fire trucks roared up. Standing about fifty feet away, they both let loose a stream of foam from their front-mounted nozzles that covered me, my plane, and the whole acre it was sitting on. I had not closed the canopy so the inside was also full of foam. I didn't care. The fire was out and my plane was still there, looking like a pile of snow.

The firemen gathered around. I had never seen a bunch of grown men so happy. As they danced around in the rain, one told me that this was the very first real aircraft fire in Phuket and they were overjoyed. This was the real thing, not a drill, and they got to use their new trucks and foam equipment—whoopee!

The airport manager called the fire chief on a cell phone and instructed me to move my plane. I pointed out that it was off the taxiway, stood only six feet high, and was way below the height of any airliner's wing. So I left it there and got a ride to the terminal with my new good friends, the Phuket Airport firemen.

I was directed to immigration officials, several of whom interrogated me for a while and released me to go to a hotel and complete all the formalities later. I told the taxi driver to take me to the closest hotel. As soon as I got to my room in the Crown Nai Yang, I telephoned my wife and then collapsed into bed.

The hotel was situated off the beach, on the east side of the peninsula on which the airport was located. The tsunami of 2004 had stripped the beachfront clean of everything on it except this hotel. It had a completely open lobby so I suppose the sea just rushed on through. I wanted to talk to the hotel personnel about the tsunami but they spoke very limited English, not enough to get any meaningful details.

The pool at the Crown Nai Yang Hotel
with tsunami-ravaged land beyond.

It seemed only moments later that the airport manager called, demanding that I come back to the airport and move my plane. I went to the security office, which issued me a crew badge so I could come and go freely. I walked to the firehouse and asked the fire chief about help and equipment to move my plane. He volunteered the whole willing crew.

We found a forklift, a cargo dolly, and some heavy rope, which I judged was all we needed. I removed the cowling and secured the rope to the engine mount. The forklift, operated by one of the firemen, lifted the plane so the dolly could be moved beneath its now-nonfunctional main wheels.

I tried to warn my friends to be careful of the brake lines in tying down the plane, but I was too late. Oh, well, I already needed new tires, wheels, and brakes—what difference would it make if new brake lines were thrown in? With the tailwheel rolling on the asphalt, the forklift tug pulled my plane down to an area the airport manager said I could use for extended parking. I shook hands with and thanked each of the firemen, who were all still quite elated.

I had called my wife before I collapsed into bed and passed on the latest news. I was a fool for mentioning the fire, because though I assured her there was no problem that couldn't be fixed with a few dollars, she called our son, John, who was living in Jakarta at the time, and told him I needed help. He in turn called a friend who ran a diving business in Phuket and asked him to help me. While I was still securing my plane, John's friend and two others appeared, offering to assist me.

The shore-based part of his business had been wiped out in the tsunami two or three months earlier. He needed help a lot more than I did, yet here he was offering to help someone he didn't even know. Generous, helpful people everywhere—I felt embarrassed. I thanked them profusely and offered lunch. They declined, no doubt to get back to restoring their business. Hell, I should have gone to help them, not the other way around.

I asked for suggestions about whom to call for aircraft parts. No luck. Concluding that I best order parts from the States, I bought an airline ticket to Jakarta to be with my son and do the ordering from there. When I showed up at the immigration desk, I forgot that I still had my crew badge around my neck.

The official there looked at my boarding pass and then my crew badge, and concluded that something was fishy. He escorted me to a nearby room, which was occupied by another uniformed official. He didn't speak English; I didn't speak Thai. I showed him my passport, in which the immigration people had written three pages in Thai that I assumed was about the accident. The official was uninterested. I tried to get him to call downstairs to those people but he either didn't want to or I didn't get the idea across to him. He kept repeating, "Tagagent." I had no idea what he meant and when I asked, he just shrugged. I later learned that the local handler's business name was Tag. The immigration guy was simply directing business to the "Tag agent," no doubt for a gratuity.

As the departure of my flight approached, I grabbed my passport and boarding pass off the desk and walked out to the boarding lounge. I sat to await the announcement. Two Thai policemen rushed up and told me I must go with them. I started to gather my camera and other possessions but they blocked my way and tugged me toward the exit. I kept asking what was going on, though I surmised it had to do with that last official. When we entered the main terminal, I stopped. The two tiny Thai policemen tried but couldn't budge me; I'm six foot two and a bit over two hundred pounds. I told them I would not go one more step until I could talk to the airport manager.

One of the policemen left and soon came back with the manager. When I told him who I was, he apologized endlessly, saying that the immigration people had made a terrible mistake. The two policemen escorted me back to the boarding lounge and I looked for my belongings. The kit with my clothes was there but my camera was missing. A Caucasian fellow whom I judged to be an American was sitting in the seat I had occupied. I asked if he had seen my camera. He neither responded nor looked at me. Angry, I told him I had just been sitting in that seat alongside the bag that remained. He still would not even acknowledge my presence.

I turned to the two Thai policemen and asked them to talk to the man about my camera. Because of his strange behavior, I now believed he had it. The police declined to intercede, whereupon I told the man that he could have the camera without prejudice if he would only give me the image card in it. That card had the photo record of my trip so far and its loss would be a crushing blow to me. The bastard never said a word and never even looked at me. I never wanted so badly to hit someone but I didn't hit him. Having just been released by the police, I thought such action might not have been terribly productive. I went away fuming to board my flight to Jakarta.

Jakarta

My son John met me at the airport and we drove to his house. I telephoned Shirley and related the items I needed from Van's to repair my plane. As I write this, I am appalled at how much I dumped on Shirley during my trip; dealing with me was almost a full-time job for her. It doesn't relieve the burden but I love her to death. After she read the list of parts back to me and some further chitchat, I retired with a cold beer to talk with my son about recent events and his business in Jakarta.

John had a partnership with a local architect in a construction venture and the business was doing quite well. In addition, he was flying for the Taiwanese and Thai governments as a helicopter search-and-rescue instructor pilot, and had participated in rescuing survivors of the tsunami in Thailand, as well as recovering the bodies of those who did not survive, a very depressing activity.

As I waited for my parts, we drove around to see some of the projects John's company was working on. Having some experience in the construction business myself, I was interested and well entertained. We also visited with Sugan, one of my son's colleagues from their earlier flying days together in Balikpapan in Borneo. Sugan had started an air-charter business in Jakarta, and was operating several airplanes based at Soekarno-Hatta International Airport. He had been approached by a Japanese group that was building large fish farms in Javanese waters and wanted Sugan to arrange to fly the fish to Japan.

With his charter business, Sugan already had all the licenses and permits, which were very hard to come by in Indonesia. Sugan and the Japanese group thought an Airbus 320 was the right plane to handle the business initially. The 320 is a European-built, passenger-and-cargo plane equivalent to the Boeing 737. The contract with the Japanese group enabled Sugan to order a 320 and hire a pilot to go to France for training. If one has the right connections in Indonesia—and connections are mandatory—there is a wealth of opportunity in that country.

We also drove with Sugan to a western seaside village that I think was Pelabuhan Ratu. Here we visited Sugan's new flash-freeze plant. Sugan and John both made a deal with local fishermen—Sugan in Pelabuhan and John in Ambon—to take unwanted fish caught by local fishermen. Fish are so plentiful in Indonesian waters that the locals get very picky about which fish they want. They catch all kinds in quantity but keep only a certain kind, discarding the rest. Sugan and John asked them for all of the fish and paid them a pittance by our standards, intending to freeze then sell the lot to the Japanese, who apparently bought all kinds of fish. Clever? I don't know, although Sugan said it was profitable.

On the drive to the west coast of Java, I was struck by the bounty of the forests. Wild bananas, papayas, coconuts, and pineapple grew everywhere. With plentiful fish in the sea, one could be poor but not hungry around here, and the weather was so mild, shelter was needed only to shed the rain and shield from the sun.

Van's Aircraft got my replacement parts to Sugan's freight forwarder in Singapore in two days. The freight forwarder had the parts in Jakarta the next day. Indonesian customs released the parts quickly—one week—thanks to special attention by

Sugan's company. I opened the boxes to inventory everything. All was there except the tires. I called Van's about them. Dale, who handled the shipment, apologized profusely for the oversight. The tires had been gathered along with everything else but inexplicably missed getting in the boxes. He promised to get them to FedEx immediately. I told him to send them to the same freight guy but this time I would pick them up in Singapore.

Since the round-trip ticket I already had required a plane change in Singapore, all I needed to do was book a flight there. John drove me to the airport, where I ran into a bit of a problem. I was carrying the box containing my spare parts, but the customs guy said I could not take it without special authorization. I explained the situation but he was adamant. He said, "Show me the invoice," to which I replied, "You know that the customs people kept the invoice."

"That is a problem for you," he said.

Knowing full well what the game was, I said, "Surely there is some way to straighten this out."

He rubbed his chin and said, "What have you for me?"

I gave him one hundred thousand rupiah. He frowned. Another hundred thousand and I still got a frown. They say the third time is the charm, so with the third hundred thousand, he smiled. Three hundred thousand rupiah, or thirty dollars, fixed my little problem. I was free to board the plane with my packages.

Upon arriving in Singapore, I bought a camera to replace the one that was "misappropriated" and then went by taxi to Hotel 88, a moderately priced hotel John used when in Singapore. The hotel was sort of like a vertical Motel 8 (everything was a high-rise in Singapore), nothing fancy but entirely adequate. The freight forwarder called the next day and delivered the tires to my hotel. I booked the next flight to Phuket. I was impressed with how well everything worked. These people were "with it."

Back in Phuket, I went directly to my plane with all my stuff. The RV-8 was parked in full view of the firehouse. Soon three firemen came over and I told the one English speaker that I had all the parts for repairs and would return at nine the next morning to get started. When I arrived as scheduled, I was not surprised to find about twelve firemen waiting to help me. Great guys.

I had built the plane so I figured I could make the necessary repairs in one day. With the help of my twelve buddies, we completed the job in a week. It was really quite a circus. But what the hell, I just couldn't tell these guys I didn't need them because they truly wanted to help, and without them, I wouldn't have even had an airplane. I was sure my buddies were good firemen but despite their eagerness, they were at a loss about what to do. Since most did not speak English, coordination of the "charging bulls" was a bit beyond my grasp.

The first thing we needed to do was jack up the plane, one side at a time, to replace the destroyed wheels. I had brought a special fixture I made to clamp onto a landing-gear leg to facilitate jacking. One of my buddies pushed me out of the way so he could help. He proceeded to install the fixture incorrectly and, with the jack, broke it. We then had to devise a different way to jack up the airplane and so it went.

Working under that blazing sun was tiring and *hot*. Although I originally thought I could make all the repairs in about a day, the work seemed never- ending. I was surprised and relieved when we finally finished. Despite the miscues, it was fun, and again, I was appreciative and proud of my firemen buddies.

I needed to do taxi testing and to do that, I needed brake fluid to make the brakes functional. I tried the Thai Airlines maintenance shop but they didn't have any. I knew I could use auto oil but not auto brake fluid because it would destroy the seals in the brakes. It was about the end of the day so I elected to quit and call the States to find out what I should do. Because of the fifteen-hour time difference, I did this through my wife.

Chuck Humphries, maintenance boss at Pacific Aircare in Watsonville, said to use vegetable oil. The next day I went shopping for corn oil, a bit of tubing, and a squirt oilcan to introduce the oil under pressure into the brake system. I found no corn oil so I settled for palm, the ubiquitous Asian cooking oil.

Back at the airport, I attached a short plastic tube to the spout of the oilcan and pumped the palm oil into my brake system. A taxi test proved the workability of cooking oil. I had thought about going to my next stop without brakes, but with the heavy load I would be carrying, I wouldn't have been able to turn the plane on the ground without brakes. I went back to the hotel, retrieved all my gear, returned to the airport, bought fuel, and bid my firemen buddies good-bye.

My destination was Johor Bahru, a city just north of Singapore. I chose it because the airport was smaller and less busy than the Singapore international one, and I thought it would be more convenient. I went to AIS to check out, thinking it would be a piece of cake. Not so. From India, I had obtained my permit for Thailand via fax and it had been easy. However, I had stated that my stay would be overnight, not the three weeks that actually resulted, so my permit covered only a one-day stay. This complicated the whole departure procedure.

Fortunately, a couple of female agents in AIS got on the phone to Bangkok and resolved the problem in a couple of hours, during which I checked out of all the other departments. When Bangkok finally cleared me, I filed an instrument flight plan with the agents, paid my five-hundred-dollar parking fee, and said good-bye to Phuket.

Johor Bahru

The flight would be short, only about five hundred miles, but the sky was so hazy, visibility was cut to about a mile or less and it got worse toward Johor Baharu. No problem, except that this again would be no sightseeing day. Arriving over Johor, I told the puzzled controller I would fly the complete instrument approach procedure on my own. The visibility really required an instrument approach, but the controller apparently thought it was a fine, clear day, with heavy haze apparently being a normal condition there.

The tower told me to park at the local flying club. On shutting down, I was greeted by two gentlemen. Captain Singh, a former airline pilot, was manager of the local flying club and Igor (last name unfortunately lost) was the Bulgarian pilot in command of an Ilyushin 76 parked nearby. It was a four-jet-engine freight hauler, really a giant bush plane capable of landing on unprepared fields with heavy loads of cargo. This particular 76 was really shabby-looking but Igor said it flew just fine.

Captain Singh offered the use of the club's maintenance hangar, another example of the ready assistance and friendship offered along the way. I quickly accepted and told him of my need for brake fluid. Their mechanic supplied me with the material. I drained out the palm oil and recharged the system with the proper stuff. I planned to stay overnight and leave for Bali early the next day. Captain Singh suggested I stay at the nearby

Sofitel Resort. I told him I had stayed at Sofitels and it strained my budget.

But it was Wednesday and they charged only forty dollars per night, he said. On the weekend the rate increased by a factor of five when Singaporeans came over to get out of their high-rise concrete jungle. This Sofitel sported a riding stable, a golf course, tennis courts, and a couple of swimming pools. The hotel itself was not quite as luxurious as the one in Dakar, but it was plenty nice and a helluva lot cheaper. I enjoyed it.

When I got back out to the airport the next day, I found that I had inadvertently left my master switch on and the battery was dead. It was the flying club to the rescue again. They charged my battery but it was so slow, I decided to stay one more night in my plush forty-dollar digs.

Bali

Checking out of the airport the next day was simple and efficient. I paid my fee of two dollars and fifty cents, had my passport stamped, and filed a flight plan for Bali. The sky was still murky but it cleared as I passed Singapore. My route would be entirely over water, down the Java Sea but not far offshore. This was one the rare times for me to do sightseeing. The sun was out, the sky was clear, and the sea was blue and beautiful. I passed several low-lying islands along the way. From my perspective, they appeared to be covered wall to wall with houses, and were only about a couple of feet above sea level. This was a disaster waiting to happen. The Indonesian tsunami was on the opposite side of the islands of Java and Sumatra, which shielded the Java Sea from its effects.

Java sits right on the "ring of fire," and accordingly has its share of the one hundred thirty or so volcanoes in Indonesia, many of which were easily visible as I flew along the Java coast. The most famous one, Krakatoa, at the northern end of Java, exploded in 1883 with a sound clearly heard in Perth, about two thousand miles away. The eruption killed about forty thousand people and dramatically changed the world's weather for nearly five years. Krakatoa, or the son of Krakatoa, was rumbling to life again, but I could not see it from my track.

I enjoyed the easy, daytime flight down the length of Java. Although I filed an instrument flight plan, air traffic control never called me once after I passed Singapore for a position report or anything else. As I approached Bali, an island just off the southern tip of Java, clouds were rapidly forming. By the time I was ready for an approach to Denpasar, the international airport on Bali, I was on instruments. I flew a bumpy approach and broke out at about four hundred feet for an easy landing.

I was directed to a parking space alongside one of the airliners. I protested, saying, "I can park on the grass at the end of the ramp." The controller wasn't having it. He insisted I park in a space for airliners, probably with airliner-sized parking fees. I gave up and did what I was told.

I was escorted into the terminal by a handler whom my son, John, had engaged. When I arrived at immigration, John was waiting for me. "Let me have the permit," I said to him. "Permit?" he asked.

It became obvious that no permit was at hand. John had volunteered in Jakarta to get the permit for me because someone on the ground in Indonesia must obtain it. I was going to use the same Syrian flight-services company, Hadid, that I used for Saudi Arabia, which had a requirement like Indonesia's. With no permit, I was at the disposal of the police. Again.

"Don't worry, Dad," John said as I was led away. "I know people in Jakarta." (Jakarta is the capital of Indonesia.) Apparently he did, because I was free to go in about an hour, being told that we would settle the permit and all the other entry details later.

John was building four houses on the beach on the southeastern side of the island, but only one was finished. It was being used by his construction crew, which he had brought down from Jakarta. John would bunk with his crew while his driver, Dewah, took me to a little hotel in Sanur, my favorite village on Bali. (Having a driver seemed at first to be a bit much, but when I saw how the Indonesians drove and found out that you could hire a driver whose weekly pay was about the price of a Starbucks coffee, it made a lot of sense.)

The hotel, Taman Agung, consisted of a main building for the reception and restaurant, about twenty-six rooms in a separate building, along with a large, tropical garden and swimming pool with lanai. The rooms were okay, but the garden and pool were lush and beautiful. There were few guests on the northwest side of Bali, as had been the case since the terrorist bombing in Kuta. As a consequence, hotel rates had dropped considerably. The charge for the week I stayed there was about one hundred dollars, including breakfast.

Pool and garden of Hotel Taman Agung in Bali.

Just across the street was a restaurant built in the traditional Balinese fashion—mostly coconut logs, giant bamboo, and straw mats with a palm-frond roof. I enjoyed the food but it was the ambiance that made this place. It was totally Balinese, including young Balinese waitresses. I ate there every night except once at an Italian restaurant, which John preferred, and one other night when I was invited to dinner by the parents of a young Balinese girl whom we were sponsoring for school in California.

John was busy with the construction of his houses, which I visited. There were two large, fairly luxurious houses, complete with bridge entrances over koi ponds and swimming pools, and two bungalows. These were intended to be rented or leased as a package, complete with cooks, maids, car, and driver. All were on a black volcanic sand beach. The setting was quite spectacular.

John had carried my wheel fairings, or wheel pants, down to Bali and to his beach houses. I had some preliminary work to do before installing them on the plane. John brought over his lead carpenter—a very clever fellow—to help me, although I was quite satisfied to work alone, remembering my helpful firemen buddies in Phuket. But John's carpenter learned very quickly and we had both wheel fairings finished in no time.

I wouldn't have bothered with new fairings except that they improve a plane's aerodynamics and consequently its range, which is obviously important over oceans. The next day the carpenter and I went out to the airport to install them. We found my plane safe and sound with two guards John had hired to protect it. I am not sure why there were two, maybe one was to keep the other awake, like the FAA tower controllers. All I had done was ask John if it was safe to leave my life raft and all my radio and navigation gear in the plane. Without notice to me, he had hired an outfit to guard my plane twenty four hours a day. He knew Bali, so I did not interfere, and the guards were probably paid the going rate—about two dollars per day. Knowing that the Balinese got so little pay, I was happy I could provide work for them.

One of the four houses John was building, taken from a similar house.

John told me the governor of the province of Ambon wanted me to fly over to the island of Ambon, the capital of the province, for an event planned to encourage tourism. The governor thought my 'round-the-world flight could add publicity to the affair. I readily agreed, as it would add a bit of spice to my trip. Ambon province consists of a number of islands, including the famous Spice Islands that the Dutch and British fought over in the seventeenth century. The Spice Islands are located in the Banda Sea, just off the west end of New Guinea.

With the governor's encouragement, John recently had established diving centers on the islands of Ambon and Banda Neira. These islands have an interesting history that touches on the motivation for European discovery from the fifteenth to the seventeenth centuries. Many know that spices such as nutmeg, cloves, and mace were extremely valuable and sought after. Few know that the big move for discovery in the world had a lot to do with spices.

Venice once controlled the spice trade into Europe by trading with Muslim traders, circa 1200 to 1500 AD. When the Turks and Mongols closed off overland routes, Venice had a monopoly on the spice trade in Europe. The Portuguese and Spanish set out to find new routes to the East to cash in on the bounty. That led to the Portuguese finally "discovering" a route to the Maluku, or Spice, Islands. The Banda Islands, a part of the Ambon province of Indonesia, were once the only source of nutmeg and mace in the world. One shipload of these spices could afford the captain and crew a lifetime retirement, even though the bulk of the riches went to the ship's owner.

Both the Portuguese and Spanish reached the Spice Islands. Conflict between them and the native population finally led to the withdrawal of the Spanish to their colony in the Philippines. The Dutch, who had been in the islands since 1599, teamed up with the natives when they rebelled against the Portuguese for trying to monopolize the spice trade. The English, a late arrival, were maneuvered out of the islands after some fighting, when the Dutch traded Manhattan for the English claims to the Spice Islands. The English, however, had an ace up their sleeves, having smuggled out spice plants for replanting in the

West Indies. This eventually led to a plentiful supply of these spices, along with a huge drop in prices. The Dutch East India Company built a fort on the island of Banda Neira, along with a number of buildings for administration and employee housing, many of which stand today as a tourist attraction and reminder of Dutch colonial times.

If I went to Ambon, I would revise my route to fly over the Spice Islands, probably landing at Banda, and visit New Guinea before proceeding to Australia. The governor was a major general in the Indonesian army, but those credentials did not allow him alone to authorize my flight to Ambon. It had to be approved by the Army headquarters in Jakarta. There had recently been bloody fighting between the Christians and Muslims on Ambon, so it was under martial law at the time and still off limits to tourism.

The islands have some of the best diving in the world and the governor, no doubt eager for revenue, wanted to open and stimulate tourism again. Unfortunately, he did not get clearance for my detour before I had to continue my trip. I was very disappointed, but I had promised the airport manager at Watsonville I would return in time for the annual fly-in and air show so I had to keep moving. I also had a side trip planned for New Zealand, one of the few countries in the world I wanted to visit and had not. I just didn't have the time to wait for the Indonesian bureaucracy to work.

My information manual told me I needed a permit for Darwin, my next destination, because the airport was joint military and civilian. The telephone system was out of service on Bali so I couldn't call, fax, or send e-mails to get the permit. I fleetingly thought of trying to contact Darwin using my HF radio before remembering that it was not operational. I had forgotten that many airports were on a special terminal network, and that I possibly could have obtained a permit through the airport. Referring to my manual, I decided to go to Broome, Australia, instead of Darwin, as Broome required no permit.

John had to leave the day before I did for his business in Jakarta, but his driver Dewah drove me out to the airport to get fuel for my flight. After the fueler had finished hand-pumping avgas out of a fifty-five-gallon drum, I counted out the requisite number of hundred-dollar bills and went about the business of checking out through all the bureaucracy.

The fuel truck came back because the office rejected most of my cash. In Indonesia—and most of Asia, I understand—U.S. currency older than two years and hundred-dollar bills with certain serial-number prefixes would not be accepted. The North Koreans have for years been pumping out counterfeit hundred-dollar bills throughout Asia. I went over to the office and asked what serial numbers they would accept. Among my stash, I found enough "good" ones to satisfy my debt.

I was all set to go except for filing a flight plan. I always left that for last because I never knew how long things would take. Usually you're allowed only so much time to take off before the flight plan is voided.

John's lead carpenter helping with wheel fairings. Bali airport.
Parked for a week in my expensive parking place along with airliners at airport's insistence. The square package in my plane is the life raft. When ditching, the canopy would be jettisoned in the air. The landing gear, upon water contact, would cause the aircraft to flip, ejecting the life raft that was tethered to the bar behind the pilot's seat, and the line attached to the inflation handle on the raft would inflate it. (This is an untested theory.)

Broome

My flight to Broome in clear sunny skies would be short, only four or five hundred miles over part of the Indian Ocean. I listened to Beethoven and Mozart on my little portable DVD player, which I had brought along for just such occasions. In clear blue skies with great music, the engine purring like a contented kitten, and the autopilot flawlessly guiding me toward the beautiful shores of Western Australia, I could not imagine a more delightful way to travel. The azure blue of the Indian Ocean yielded to bright turquoise near the seemingly endless white sands of Cable Beach, just west of Broome.

Since it was such a short overwater trip and there was no need to conserve fuel, I set power for one hundred eighty knots and arrived in just over three hours. As I flew over the peninsula on which the city was located, toward the bay beyond, the air traffic controller told me to orbit until further notice. Orbit was the Australian/English term for the American word "hold." It all meant flying around in circles for a while. I could see the airport clearly and saw only one aircraft operation—a plane taking off—and wondered why I had to orbit so far away. As a matter of fact, it was only the second plane I had seen in flight during my trip up to that point. Both were light twins, one over the Sierras after leaving Watsonville, and this one. I'd heard lots of airliners on the radio but had seen only those two.

The Broome controller called me to land and asked if I had notified customs, to which I said no. When I landed, the controller asked if I could see a little green shack at the edge of the airport. When I said yes, he told me to park by it and stay with the airplane. I did that, shut down, and got out to stretch my legs.

After a while, a rotund, red-faced Aussie and two women came along. The man announced, "I am the customs officer. You have committed an offense against the laws of Australia. You have the right to remain silent. Anything you say will be taken down and used in a court of law against you…"

I could not suppress a grin as I asked, "What offense did I commit?"

He scowled, saying, "You failed to notify customs."

"My information manual tells me that Broome is an international airport and that notification is not necessary."

"It is in Broome. Let me see your passport and visa."

"Here's my passport but I don't have a visa. I'm American aircrew making a technical stop in Darwin for repairs and therefore do not need a visa, as I understand the rules."

"You are wrong. You have the right to remain silent. Anything you do say will be taken down and used in a court of law…" He repeated that whole bit.

The customs officer went through my plane and found the large plastic bag in which I stored receipts and other papers documenting payments so far on my trip. Removing the papers from the bag, he carelessly tossed them onto the tarmac, scattering many to the stiff winds. I was surprised he didn't cite me for littering.

Meanwhile the women, botanical and health inspectors, searched all the interior corners of my plane and asked if I had it fumigated in Bali. I told them I had not and they never mentioned the subject again. (Some weeks after returning home, I received several bills from Australia, one of which was for fumigating my airplane, which never occurred.)

The man, now holding a small wooden carving I had bought in India for three dollars, said, "You did not declare this! You have the right to remain silent. Anything you say will be taken down…" That whole thing again.

I said, "It completely slipped my mind."

He said, "I will have to call Canberra to find out what disposition will be made of you." (Canberra, as you probably know, is the capital of Australia.)

The telephone was on the outside wall of the green shack so I could hear everything he said. He enumerated all my "offenses," told them what I had said, and then listened a couple of minutes before saying, "He is? He can? Damn!" He came back, obviously unhappy, and said, "You are free to go, but you can only stay a month!" I think his disappointment had a lot to do with the fact that he didn't get to see this Yank in jail.

I gathered up all the papers I could, cursing the customs guy under my breath because those papers were important records of my trip. I called a taxi and asked to be taken to the closest hotel at the discretion of the cabbie. The hotel/motel and bar had the feeling of an old-time Western outpost, which I guess it really was. I had a couple of Foster's beers and, like Crocodile Dundee, said "g'day" to some folks, had dinner, and then retired to bed.

Darwin

The flight to Darwin the next day along the shoreline was routine and pleasant. Who gets tired of being at the beach or flying over it? The weather was good, the sun was out, and the landscape sometimes looked like western Texas. It was a desert in stark contrast to the blue of the Indian Ocean. There were many bays along the way, and eventually a big expanse of water that was an extension of the Timor Sea. That water crossing was more than three hundred miles.

Then I flew over Fannie Bay to reach Darwin International Airport. The grounds were quite expansive, like all of Australia. It seemed like I had to taxi forever to reach the part of the airport dedicated to general aviation. The general-aviation ramp was located at the northwest end, the airline terminal at the northeast, and the military (RAAF) one at the Southern southern part of the field.

I taxied to Phoenix Aviation, which was adjacent to NT Electronics, both of which I needed. I wanted a mechanic to carefully check my engine to make sure it was okay for the Pacific crossing, and I needed a new high-frequency antenna to replace the one ripped off in the Brazilian thunder storm. Fortunately, the general-aviation area was within walking distance of the Darwin Airport Resort where I was to stay.

On entering Phoenix's office the next day, I saw a bald fellow at the counter and concluded that he must be Dean Stahr. I had been told that Dean would be flying around the world in his Cessna 182RG, traveling westward. I had never met him but had talked with him via telephone several months earlier when a mutual friend, Jack Reichel, told me about Dean's plan.

At first, we had both planned to go eastward up through Iceland, and talked of flying together at least on the legs from Goose Bay via Reykjavik to Scotland. Beyond that, Dean was afraid I couldn't keep up with his 182, which can cruise at about one hundred fifty-five knots. Dean didn't finish his planning in time for the summer crossing—he was a meticulous planner—and I didn't finish building and testing my RV-8.

Speaking of planning, Dean spent months planning his trip, had mountains of charts, and real-time communications via satellite phone with a retired airline captain back in Arizona who acted as "mission control." The captain would monitor weather in real time and advise Dean to deviate this or that way or delay takeoff entirely. A Canadian flight-services company handled flight-planning and other details. Later Dean accused me of simply wetting my finger and sticking it into the air to plan for my trip. I did a bit more than that but nowhere near what he did.

I learned of Dean's planned stop in Darwin from Jack via my nightly phone calls to Shirley. After we became acquainted, we went about our separate business transactions, agreeing to meet at Phoenix Aviation when we were all done. I found the electronics specialist and arranged for him to repair and test my high-frequency radio. I so far had finessed its inoperable state, but I knew the Aussies would check it out before departing Australia. I told the manager at Phoenix that I wanted a mechanic to change the oil and look for "show stoppers" in my engine since I would be flying over eight thousand miles of the Pacific. Dean wanted a hundred-hour inspection done on his plane.

After finishing our business, we walked over to the Darwin Airport Resort. It was a newly-opened hotel and I found it to be superior. We had been told that the work on our planes would take two days, so we were free to lounge around the pool, eat, and drink to our hearts' content. Dean was fun to be with and the hotel satisfied all our needs. On our last night in Darwin, we had dinner in the hotel's restaurant and spent our time telling flying stories, some of which may have been true.

An attractive woman sitting at an adjacent table overheard our talk about flying, and announced that she too was a pilot flying for a charter operator. After a short banter, she asked if she could join us. "Why not?" said Dean. The three of us talked flying for a while, finished dinner, and were enjoying an after-dinner drink when our new friend began to make an aggressive play for Dean, saying, "You are gorgeous." Dean was seventy-nine, bald, slightly overweight, and she was about forty, attractive, and slim. I was amused by the scene, mainly her approach to Dean, and I thought, "Better him than me." (When we met at Jack Reichel's house after returning home, I told the story to Jack but Dean said it was me, not him.) I decided that I ought to vanish to bed. I don't know how long Dean stayed up that night and he wouldn't say. Since we both had to fly early the next day, I trust it was not too late.

Next morning, when I visited Phoenix Aviation to pay my bill, the mechanic told me he had found that one of the plugs in the bottom of the oil sump was only finger tight. There were a total of five plugs on the sump, two were safety-wired, and the others were supposed to be permanently sealed at the factory. Had he not found that loose plug, it could well have vibrated off, I would have lost all engine oil, and a couple of minutes later the engine would have seized and quit running, possibly while I was out there somewhere over the Pacific. I properly expressed my gratitude to the mechanic. When you think about it, aircraft mechanics undergo extensive training, must be certified and licensed, work on difficult, complicated machines, and save lives every day, yet are paid half the wages of auto mechanics. I am especially appreciative since one of the lives saved was mine.

I bid farewell to Dean, who was off to Jakarta. Following my Internet posting about the bureaucracy in India, Dean had revised his route to skip India, planning to fly from Phuket to Sri Lanka and then directly to Oman.

Darwin Airport Resort, where Dean and I stayed. Great place.

Cairns

My next stop was Cairns, Australia, on the northeastern shore near the Great Barrier Reef. The flight was roughly one thousand nautical miles (eleven hundred fifty statute miles). Three hundred miles of that leg was over the Gulf of Carpenteria. I now had an affinity for water.

Cairns International Airport hides behind a long, high hill when approached from the west, making it a fun approach. You round the hill and there it is. It was a domestic flight so no hassle. When I arrived, I was careful to check in with customs since I did not want a repeat of the Broome disaster. The customs officer I talked with was the kind of Aussie I had known and liked. With a friendly smile, he said, "Hell, mate, you don't have to check in here. Just photocopy your main passport page and general declaration form and fax them to us. And you can file your flight plan by phone or fax." Yeah, that was the kind of Aussies I had known in the past. Australia had been part of my territory when I was in the corporate world. I had spent a fair amount of time there and liked the country and the people very much.

I chose to stay at the Shangri-la Hotel, located at the marina in downtown Cairns, a perfect spot with sunshine, boats and water. What more could a wandering pilot want? Additionally, the water side of the bath in my room had a glass wall so I could look at the nautical scenery even while showering. I liked it so much I decided to stay two days. I had access to the Internet at the hotel so I used it to communicate with my son and my wife. I also thanked my wild Italian friend for a great visit in Rome, and answered numerous e-mails from both friends and strangers from all over the world wishing me good luck on my flight. I even received an e-mail from a soldier in Iraq wishing *me* luck. I answered, properly pointing out that he was the one who needed the luck.

Walking around Cairns, I decided I wouldn't mind at all living there. It was a neat little town. As much as I wanted to stay, I had obligations to meet and scheduled my departure for the next day, using the fax to accomplish all of the departure procedures as suggested by the friendly airport official. Unfortunately, I calculated that I no longer had sufficient time left to visit New Zealand so had to scratch that detour.

On the deck of the Shangri La Hotel in Cairns. Tough duty.

New Caledonia

The next morning, not too early (Cairns relaxes you), I launched into the cloudy skies for the fourteen-hundred-nautical-mile crossing to La Tontouta, New Caledonia, over the Great Barrier Reef. I steered south of a direct route, almost to Mackay, to get a broader view of the reef system. The sun shone past the broken clouds to highlight the thousand shades of blue and emerald that was the Coral Sea. I saw numerous small islands rising with their white coral shores above the turquoise waters. I am not a diver but this sight could have induced me to become one. I was thoroughly enjoying the view when the Brisbane controller called to inquire about my destination and intentions. I apologized for drifting off course, telling him the reason, to which he said, "It's awraat, mite. It's a gryt saight, innit?" I told him I would regain my track for New Caledonia and switch over to HF. He said, "G'day. 'ave a nyss flyt."

I called radio Brisbane, reported in, and repeated my intent to intercept my original track. The clouds ahead did not look as picturesque and friendly as they had earlier. Nevertheless, I was headed for New Caledonia. Captain Cook "discovered" it in 1774 and, as the English were inclined to do, renamed the island. Caledonia was the old Latin name for Scotland, so the "newly discovered" island was named New Caledonia.

During WWII, Nouméa, with its harbor, was headquarters for the U.S. Navy and an advanced staging base for operations in the Pacific. I remember it from newsreels and other wartime reports. The people on the island had dreaded the advance of the Japanese and were glad when the Americans decided to establish a base there. I am told that they still remember the Americans with fondness which I believe was demonstrated during my visit there. After the war the islands reverted to their status as a French colony. A vote will take place in the next four or five years to determine whether the population wants to be independent or remain with France. I will be quite interested in how that turns out, and I am sure my French friends on the island will be as well.

Contrary to the forecast, the cloudy skies turned stormy and quite dark as I approached La Tontouta. Forecasts in the U.S. are designed to last about twelve hours and sometimes do. In the tropics, forecasts are good for about as long as it takes to issue them. That was one reason I always tried to file instrument flight plans. If the weather turned sour, I would still be good to go if the change was not too severe.

Rain began pelting my canopy as I entered the clouds at seven thousand feet. They were big drops and sounded like BB's hitting the windscreen. I assumed that the approach to La Tontouta would be on instruments so I retrieved the approach plate for the ILS. I decided that I was probably going to land at La Tontouta no matter what the weather did. There is no alternate airport within a reasonable distance so I concluded that my best alternative to not landing was to return to Australia. It was not an uplifting proposition as it would be a thirteen or fourteen hour round trip although I did have the fuel to do it. I picked up the HF mic to ask Radio Brisbane to check the current weather at La Tontouta but nixed the idea when I realized I was going to fly the approach anyway.

Turbulence was light to moderate as I contacted La Tontouta and was told that the ceiling was "right around one hundred feet and dropping" and the visibility "half mile or less." This brought back memories of the blind landing at Belem and my heart rate quickened. The Brazilian affair more or less sneaked up on me but this time I had a lot of time to think about it. I knew I was gambling but resolved to continue. I told the controller that I would self navigate the approach for the ILS and he didn't object. (thinking about it later I concluded that they didn't even have approach radar and that self navigation is a must.)

There being no traffic in the area, I was unhurried in my approach and I took my time to get it right. I slowed to ninety knots, configured my plane for landing and positioned myself to intercept the localizer using my GPS. With the Jeppesen approach plate clipped to my knee board, I displayed the approach procedure on my Garmin 430 and tuned the ILS frequency on my number two navigation radio. All alone under a rain swept canopy, unable to see anything outside, approaching a place I knew nothing about over an endless expanse of water in a small single engine airplane with virtually no ceiling and extremely limited visibility, it all seemed surreal. Despite some anxiety, I thought, "this

Is what I came for."

Having intercepted the localizer, I advised the controller of the fact and continued toward the airport scanning my instruments anticipating glide slope intercept. Once accomplished, I slowed slightly and adjusted my descent rate to match and proceeded very carefully to avoid dropping below the glide slope (down where the rocks are). I was anticipating a further drop in the ceiling and was prepared to deal with it no matter how low it might be. I was concentrating so hard no extraneous thoughts could penetrate. The faintest hint of a deviation of either needle on the CDI brought my instant correction. I had to get this right.

When I reached one hundred feet I could still see nothing. I refreshed my mind with the first step in the missed approach procedure, although I still intended to go lower. I could almost hear my heartbeat as I glanced up looking for any sign of the airport. A couple of seconds later I caught a blurry flash of the runway lights through the rain spattered windscreen. I felt the wheels touch gently. With a sign of relief, I thought "not a bad landing". For the first time I realized I was all wet, not from the rain, but from perspiration during the approach. I taxied to the ramp and shut down.

As usual in the rain, I got soaked getting out of my plane. I ran to the terminal but it wasn't open so I banged on the door and waited in the rain—there was no porch or overhang—for someone to respond. Thankfully, one of the officials was still there and opened up for me. The trip took longer than I had planned because of the weather and the detour toward Mackay, and the tight instrument approach added still more time.

I cleared all the arrival formalities and went back out to my plane, intending to fly just off the water to the Nouméa Magenta airport since I had booked a hotel room in Nouméa. The rain had stopped and I took off but stayed below the cloud deck, which meant I was about fifty feet over the water in low visibility, planned planning to "scud run" to Nouméa. The visibility had decreased since I landed, and I quickly decided I was on a fool's errand, so I climbed to two thousand feet into the clouds over the water and made another instrument approach into La Tontouta. When I landed, the controller said, "That was a wise decision." He could have added "to end that stupid trip to disaster." I stayed in a little local inn called Tontoutel, and by chance the telephones worked so I called my Shirley to report for the day.

Next morning, it was still raining. I did not have an instrument-approach plate for the Nouméa Magenta airport, located about forty miles away. But it had only one non-precision approach, and the procedure was in the database of my Garmin 430. The weather at Magenta was reported as a ceiling of eight hundred feet and visibility of one mile in the rain. I decided to go so I got soaked again and took off on an instrument flight plan. Offshore near Magenta, I let down to marginal visual flight conditions at five hundred feet and made a visual approach.

As I taxied in, I noticed two fellows motioning for me to go over to a hangar whose door was open. I did as directed, shut down the engine, and they pushed my plane into the hangar. The two men turned out to be French citizens: Captain Hugues Jurion, retired Air France; and Dr. Jacques-Florian Letourneulx, an anesthesiologist. We parked my plane next to a North American AT-6, a WWII-era advanced trainer jointly owned by Hugues and Jacques.

Hugues is a smiling, friendly, outgoing fellow who is fun to be around. Jacques is more reserved than Hugues but is also welcoming and generous. Both are a credit to France and New Caledonia.

Hugues guided me to his car and off we went to a nice, seaside restaurant for lunch. The sun had come out by this time and I could appreciate the beautiful setting. Hugues and I had a lengthy lunch, all the while exchanging information on backgrounds. Hugues was born in France and had served as a fighter pilot in the French Air Force. During his combat training, while flying a Fouga jet, another pilot collided with him, tearing off a wing. He successfully bailed out and got another colorful tale to tell. He went on to fly supersonic jet fighters. Once discharged, he signed on with Air France and in due course became Captain. In France he lived just outside of Paris, and he and his wife Michele decided to retire on the beautiful island of New Caledonia.

After lunch, Hugues drove me to my hotel, the Novotel, which was perhaps the only high-rise in Nouméa. He called shortly after I checked in and told me that he would pick me up for a dinner party at Jacques's house that Jacques had arranged. The house was located near the top of a high ridge overlooking the beautiful harbor and the city of Nouméa. Jacques and his lovely wife, Giaette, were at the party, along with Hugues and his beautiful wife, Michele, and a lawyer and his wife. (I did record the lawyer's name but unfortunately it has been lost.) It was a wonderful party and I enjoyed it immensely. The only problem for me was that most of the conversation was in French and spoken too fast. I had lived in the French-speaking part of Belgium, but my long work hours precluded me from becoming fluent in French. Plus, that had been thirty-six years earlier.

The following day, Hugues picked me up at the hotel and we went to the airport. I told Hugues I had owned an AT6 when I was seventeen years old, about sixty years earlier. Hugues immediate response was to ask if I would like to fly his airplane – generous fellow that he is.. I had thought the AT6 was the greatest airplane in the world. My memory of it was as an agile, aerobatic, and thoroughly romantic bird. However, after flying my highly sensitive, quick, and delightfully harmonized RV-8, my evaluation of the AT-6 was downgraded quite a bit. (I did not tell Hugues. He was building an RV-8 of his own at the time of this writing so he will would soon find out for himself.)

After we returned and landed, we encountered Dominique Levrel, another local pilot and a colonel in the French Army. He owned a CAP 10, a French sport plane. Soon, Dominique's pretty young wife—all the French women in Nouméa seemed to be pretty—came along and decided we should have a party at their house. Later that day we all gathered at Dominique's house for drinks and, well, mostly drinks. I don't know about the others but I had a very good time.

I had planned to stay only overnight in Nouméa, but the warm hospitality of these Frenchmen induced me to stay another day. My prior experience, mostly in Paris, had left me with some antipathy toward the French, or at least their attitude toward Americans. This New Caledonia experience certainly put all that to rest.

Early the next morning, my new friend Hugues picked me up at the hotel and drove to the airport tower and administrative building. I tried to get clearance to depart New Caledonia from Magenta, but the officials there told me I would have to fly back to La Tontouta, the only international airport on New Caledonia, to obtain a clearance. I told them that my plane was fully fueled (there was no fuel in La Tontouta) and loaded, and I could not risk landing with all that weight. I was especially concerned about the tailwheel and its attachment arm. "Then perhaps you will stay in New Caledonia," one of the officials said.

My French friends went to work on these bureaucrats and straightened them out. They relented and said I could fax the information over to La Tontouta "but you still cannot leave."

"Why not?"

"Because air traffic control is going on strike...now!"

Hugues, my personal French cavalry, was back to the rescue. After he worked them over, the officials said if I could contact Fiji—my next destination—on my aircraft radio, I could go.

We drove over to the other side of the field where my plane was located, all the while doubting that contact from mountainous New Caledonia to Fiji was in the cards. I pushed my plane away from the hangar into the open and called on my HF radio. "Radio Nadi, this is November eight seven eight delta zulu. Do you read?" I was astounded to hear, "Eight delta zulu, this is Radio Nadi, go ahead." I yelled to Hugues, who was sitting in the cockpit of his AT-6 and in radio contact with the tower. "Hugues, I raised Radio Nadi!" (Nadi is pronounced Nandi. It seems that in the Melanesian and Polynesian islands, the "n" in names is pronounced but not written. Example: Pago Pago is pronounced Pango Pango.)

Hugues talked with the tower then got out and walked over to my plane. It turned out that I still couldn't go until all the air traffic control personnel had left the government buildings, so that they would not have any responsibility for me. Responsible for what, I do not know, as there was no radar coverage for the route (or, I don't think, even locally) and there wasn't any traffic. The ATC people were on strike but didn't show any urgency about leaving. Well, we waited until after noon.

Hugues and Jacques decided to fly formation with me for a while toward Fiji. I was honored to have these great people give me this send-off. Nouméa was without doubt the highlight of my trip, and I shall always remember these people fondly. Vive la Calédonie!

Capt. Hugues Jurion (Air France) & Col. Dominique Levrel (French Army).

Nouméa, New Caledonia.

Hugues and Jacques escorting me part way to Fiji.

Fiji And Pago Pago

I took off first and that was a mistake, because my airplane was faster than the AT-6. Also, I should have made a larger-radius turn to allow them to form up. Good pilot that he was, Hugues got on my right wing in echelon anyway. And away we flew for the next hour. When he had to turn back toward Magenta, Hugues rocked his wings and I did also. Jacques took a photo of my RV-8 flying off in the gathering dusk toward Fiji.

It was getting dark as I landed at Nadi. The delays, long flight, parties with my new friends, and lack of sleep left me feeling quite tired as I climbed out of the cockpit.

I had visited Nadi once before, in 1971, on the inaugural Qantas 747 flight from San Francisco to Sydney. After leaving Honolulu, and being airborne for about three hours, we had a fire in the starboard outboard engine. The engine was shut down and the crew decided to make a precautionary landing at Nadi. At that time there was no terminal or any other passenger facilities there, just a large Quonset hut. A 747 load of passengers deplaned with nowhere to go and nothing to do, not even a place to sit down except on the ground.

Frankly, I don't know why the captain didn't proceed to Sydney, which was imminently feasible in a three-engine 747. Recently a British Airways 747 lost an engine over Nevada after leaving Los Angeles and proceeded all the way to London on three engines. Maybe it was because the Quantas plane was so new. We were told that we would wait in Nadi for a new engine to be brought over from someplace. Qantas arranged for the passengers to stay in private homes until the plane could be made ready to go three days later.

Two other fellows and I were assigned to a simple, airy little bungalow. I didn't mind at all—just a little more color. For something to do, I walked into the town of Nadi, which was very small then, and managed to talk to some of the black Fijians. They told me they were very unhappy with the government and the Indians who seemed to run everything with the backing of the government. (Later, if memory serves me correctly, there was some violence in Fiji among the ethnic groups.)

This second time around, in 2005, Nadi had a large new airport and fairly new terminal. Arriving at immigration with my uniformed escort, I was asked for my entry permit. "Aha! I checked carefully before I left and found that I do not need a permit or visa for Fiji." But I had left the States on March 9 and the rules changed on April 1. It never occurred to me to recheck everything enroute.

The immigration people were adamant, saying that while I didn't need a visa, I simply could not stay without an entry permit. More precisely, *I* could stay but my airplane couldn't. I asked to talk to the airport manager. It was Sunday and he was not there. I insisted that they try to find him and they very reluctantly made a few phone calls, or at least they said they did.

Three hours passed and still no results in locating the manager. I asked what I should do in the event we could not locate him. The senior officer present said, "Just fly on." I had not slept well the previous night, ; the parties, the bureaucracy, the long flight, and the standing around left me very tired. It was already eight p.m. so I thought I ought to get going while I could still operate my plane. I had no opportunity to file a flight plan but hoped to do it in the air with the tower. Unfortunately, they declined.

After takeoff I tried to contact Pago Pago via HF radio but had no luck. (HF is quirky. Sometimes you have no trouble contacting someone five thousand miles away, and sometimes you can't raise anyone close by. I later learned the reason I couldn't raise anyone in Pago Pago was nobody was manning the radios.) The weather was okay but the skies were cloudy and it was another of those black, black nights. For the first and only time, I had trouble staying awake in the air. The flight seemed like torture, mostly because of the fatigue and my disappointment over being turned away from Fiji. After all, how many parties, late nights, long flying hours, and rejections can a seventy-six-year-old geezer stand?

This leg was a little less than a thousand miles but it seemed to take forever. It was actually only seven hours or so. Nearing Pago Pago, I called approach control. No answer. I called the tower. No reply. Then I heard a Hawaiian Airlines pilot on the ground alerting airborne traffic that he was taking off. We coordinated his departure and then my arrival through low, broken clouds.

I flew a very precise instrument approach but like in Dakar, I saw only a big black area when I should have been seeing runway lights. I flew a missed approach. (Remember, it was designed to keep planes away from weeds and rocks and there were lots of *big* rocks in Pago Pago.) Then I came around for another approach, deciding I would have to land, lights or no lights, and my feeble landing light was no help. Lo and behold, the runway lights came on as I was on final approach. Once on the ground, I learned that one of the security staff turned on the lights after hearing me fly by on the missed approach. I was very grateful because this weary old pilot needed all the help he could get.

The ground staff—security, immigration, customs, and health—was still around, having just checked out the Hawaiian Airlines passengers. I checked in with them and told my story about Fiji. I chatted with the guys for a while and then they apologized and locked me in a room. Since I had not been able to contact Pago Pago from Fiji or enroute, nobody knew I was coming. Pago Pago is part of American Samoa. TSA (Transportation Security Administration) procedures had been established, and, not having notified TSA in advance, I was in trouble.

After an hour or so, the airport manager, a short, rotund woman who had been roused from bed, arrived at the airport, apparently pretty well steamed. I was told later by one of the immigration fellows that since I had not complied with TSA rules, she was adamant that I should not be allowed to stay. Security, immigration, customs, health, and the airport manager eventually had a vote and it came out three to two in my favor. I had no idea what I would have done if they had told me to fly on. I thanked my lucky stars that I had made friends with the immigration, customs, and security guys, for theirs were the votes that allowed me to stay.

Security called a taxi for me and I went to the nearest hotel, the Tradewinds. I collapsed into bed and slept until three that afternoon. I hurriedly dressed, went to the airport to have my plane fueled, and checked it over for the next leg to Christmas Island. It was in the Republic of Kiribati, which includes Howland Island, where Amelia Earhart was headed when she disappeared. I was impressed to see a seemingly vertical mountain rise up close to the airport. Good reason to fly a careful approach and a precise missed approach.

I went back to the hotel, called Shirley to bring her up to date, had dinner, and slept some more. My calls to my wife were often made at times of opportunity without regard to time-zone differences. She insisted this was fine, but I know she lost a lot of sleep because of the erratic timing of my calls, and I greatly appreciated her spirit and helpfulness. I rose early next morning and went to the airport. Nobody was around, not security or the air traffic control people. I couldn't file a flight plan or anything else, so I just took off for Christmas Island.

Preparing to depart Pago Pago for Christmas Island.

Christmas Island

After takeoff, I tried air-filing a flight plan by HF radio but could not raise Christmas Island. This leg was fourteen hundred nautical miles (sixteen hundred statute). Add in climb and approach time, it would require about ten hours. The weather was good, I listened to Beethoven, and the time passed quickly, despite the fact the scenery didn't change a hell of a lot.

Approaching my destination, I tried again and this time the island came back with a welcome and a scolding for having not filed a flight plan. After all, airplanes arrived there every month or two, and to not know when one was coming was unforgivable from an air traffic controller's point of view. "With all that traffic, dangerous conditions could exist if ATC isn't fully informed, right?" the controller asked.

From the air, the island looked a shambles, with bomb-like craters over much of it. I landed on a rough runway and taxied over an even rougher ramp to a ramshackle, old building sporting a sign: WELCOME TO CHRISTMAS ISLAND. The radio operator/air traffic controller/customs officer/fueler/airport manager came out of his little shack and greeted me. He was a bit agitated that no one had told him I was coming, but he quickly regained what I would later learn was his normal state—happy and laughing. He also mentioned that the telephones had been out for about two months but that was no problem. It happened all the time.

He called together his two fuel guys and they hand-pumped avgas from a fifty-five-gallon drum into my plane. (Fuel was sold in drums only, at more than six hundred dollars per drum. Need more than one but not quite two? Pay for two and leave the remainder behind.) I looked at the fuel in the drum before I let them put any in. It looked clean and the interior of the drum looked new.

It was important to check on the availability of avgas on Christmas Island. I had read about a fellow who did not and had to remain there two months for fuel to arrive. It must have been exciting. I knew about it being sold in drum quantities only so I planned my fuel usage to require just one drum when I got there. The island attracts bone fishermen from the U.S. and probably other places during bone-fishing season. Most of the fishermen come in private planes and that is why avgas exists at all there.

The name of the airport guy who did everything was Ueata Tetab. He stated it twice but I still have no idea how to pronounce it. He was lighthearted, helpful, and generally colorful. I took his photo but it did not turn out well. He told me, with a big smile, of course, "Don't show my picture to the women in the States because they will all come over here looking for me," and then burst into laughter. The gas truck gave me a ride to the Captain Cook Hotel, the only lodging on the island.

I found the staff at the hotel, like the airport man, to be happy and seemingly carefree. I wondered how they got that way. These people had nothing except what the ocean and some puny palm trees gave them. Perhaps it was the radiation. The British dropped an atom bomb on the island in 1956, according to my IFIM. They moved the inhabitants off, dropped the bomb, and a couple of weeks later, moved the people back onto the island.

"Passenger terminal" on Christmas Island.

The best thing one can say about the Captain Cook Hotel is that it keeps the rain out. I was taken to my room, and, having gotten up early and flown all day, I needed the bathroom. Properly relieved, I discovered there was no toilet paper. No matter, I thought, I will just jump into the shower. I guess I was getting less observant. There was no towel, no soap. I thought the blower on the low, window-mounted air conditioner would help me dry off. The A/C rumbled to life, sounding like a D-8 bulldozer, and I thought that melody ought to be great for sleeping.

As the only guest, I would be dining alone. Happily they had scotch whiskey, affording me a brief happy hour before dinner. They served me the only item available: fish. It was pretty good, although I had no idea what kind of fish it was. I went to bed early and found that my bulldozer air conditioner actually had cooled the room a bit, which was highly desirable since Christmas Island is right on the equator. I tried to sleep through the clatter but only half managed it.

It started to rain before daylight and soon it became a deluge, sounding like a herd of horses on the metal roof. The rain was accompanied by thunder and lightning so I knew I wouldn't be flying right away. Nevertheless, I rose early, had breakfast, and talked the hotel staff into giving me a ride to the airport. (I couldn't telephone.) I had arranged with Ueata Tetab to meet me at the airport at seven a.m., and I suspected he would slog through the downpour to be there. I didn't need him but he needed to be there—a sense of duty. The airport ramp was ankle deep in water, and right at seven along came my man on his bicycle, plowing through the rain and standing water. He was smiling broadly, as if to say every minute of every day was beautiful, even under water.

I told him we could do any and all paperwork then so he would not have to come back to the airport later. He wouldn't have it. After all, among all the other things, he was the airport manager and couldn't leave the airport unattended while aircraft operations were going on. We agreed to return when the rain had passed. I returned to the hotel in their truck and whiled away the morning reading.

After lunch at about one p.m., the storm passed and I hitched another ride out to my plane. Mr. Happy was there and ready to formally check me out. I handed him my flight plan, knowing full well that it was a dead letter because the power was out, and without power it was going nowhere. He performed his official duties with great solemnity and flourish, after which he broke into gales of laughter. I wish I had his spirit around all the time.

Hawaii

I took off on the twelve-hundred-nautical-mile flight to Kona on the big island of Hawaii. I tried to call there on HF but got no response after several tries. The weather on Christmas Island was fair when I left, but soon the skies became filled with dark cumulus clouds, which I did not want to see. I deviated to the west to get around the worst-looking of the lot, but it soon got nasty anyway. Possibly the weather had something to do with my being unable to contact Kona. It was late when I left and the detour added some time to the trip so it was dark when I arrived. I flew my customary ILS approach and taxied to a spot the ground controller specified.

I had to clear U.S. TSA, customs, and immigration. In years past, I had not had very good luck with these people, and I dreaded dealing with them now as I had forced them, without prior notification, to get out of bed and return to the airport. I steeled myself for an unpleasant encounter.

After about an hour, two men arrived, and to my great surprise, they were smiling. The lead man, Henry, introduced them both and offered his hand in a truly welcoming handshake. Aloha is real. I was dumbfounded. Soon, I learned that Shirley had been in almost daily contact with them about my impending arrival. It was clever of her. She correctly assumed, since sometimes telephone service was unavailable, that I might not have been able to contact them. Her call had made friends for me, and I am truly grateful. I think I will have her call ahead on all my future returns to the U.S., whether by private plane or on an airline. Hawaii's was the slickest clearance I had ever had with U.S. Customs and TSA. It wasn't like in Pago Pago, where I also didn't file a flight plan or announce my arrival in advance. As I write this, it occurs to me that I must also have penetrated an ADIZ (air defense identification zone) in Hawaii. Unlike in Greece, nothing happened here.

I remained in Kona overnight and planned to fly to Oahu the next day to visit old friends. I had damaged one of the wheel pants by running into an inoperable taxi light, three of which had been placed in a triangular pattern in the middle of the taxiway at a two-way turn. I repaired it with duct tape, well enough for it to hold together and be fairly aerodynamic. Never fly without duct tape.

I flew over to the international airport at Honolulu. I called my friends and got directions to their place in Kailua on the northeastern side of the island. I rented a car and drove over the beautifully scenic highway.

My friends, the Kobaras, have a beautiful place on the mountainside overlooking the Pacific and some offshore islands. A magnificent place to live and the weather wasn't bad, either. They graciously entertained me for several days until my air-show commitment forced me to move on. I said good-bye to my dear friends, booked a hotel room near the Honolulu International Airport (it was about five miles away), and planned to leave about midnight in order to arrive in California during the day. It would be truly gratifying to land someplace in the daytime, as I knew Shirley and a couple of friends wanted to meet me.

I took a taxi to the airport, went to my plane, and found it had a flat tire. Damn. I needed at least a jack and a compressor, which I did not have. There was nothing to do but go back to the hotel and try to get some sleep. I couldn't get a taxi so I had to walk. Didn't mind it but it took a lot of time, of which I was now short. I called Shirley to let her know my departure was delayed then went back to bed.

I had to get up midmorning to repair my tire. I saw a fellow in an open hangar working on an airplane I identified as a Van's RV-3. That gave us something important in common. I introduced myself as the owner of the RV-8 on the ramp. He identified himself as Gene Wilkie and immediately asked if there was anything he could do for me. I briefly told him my story and what I needed. We tried the compressor but the tire would not hold air. He called around, found a friend who had an inner tube of the correct size, and I bought it. My new friend installed the tube and remounted the tire. He left me with nothing to do but watch. The pilots I met on my trip were all like that—eager to help and quick to offer.

Just before completing reinstallation of the brakes, Gene said, "I have to go fly, just finish tightening these bolts." (He was a UPS pilot who flew freight around the Hawaiian Islands.) I tightened the bolts he had already inserted in the brake-pad retainer, checked over the plane for airworthiness, then returned to the hotel, hoping to get a little sleep before having to rise at ten p.m. to start my journey home. I have trouble sleeping when my schedule get all screwed up and going to bed late afternoon to get up mid evening is all screwed up.

Back at the airport, I started the engine, and after a brief warm-up, performed the ground checks on the engine and airframe. I called ground control for taxi clearance and found that I couldn't turn the plane to the right. When the plane is fully loaded for an oceanic crossing, I need brakes to initiate a turn, and the right brake, the one Gene and I had worked on, was not working. I considered going ahead, but reasoned that I might not be able to get on the runway making only left turns. Such a caper would have been illegal anyway.

Canceling my taxi clearance, I returned to my parking place and shut down. After removing the wheel pant and examining the brake, I discovered that my friend had not slipped the brake pad over the disk. Like a fool, I had simply taken up where he left off and tightened the bolts on an improperly installed and now nonfunctional brake. By the time I remedied all that and tested the brake, something I should have done the day before, I concluded it was too late to depart and still meet my requirement of arriving in daylight.

So, back to the hotel (at least I was getting a lot of exercise walking), where I called my Shirley to explain the delay once more. I told her I would depart at eleven thirty Hawaiian time and arrive at four thirty California time, but she shouldn't bother trying to meet me. "I'll call you from the Watsonville airport," I said. Then I went back to bed as the sun came up.

My circadian clock was all messed up and I couldn't sleep so I got up and went to the airport. At least I got a ride. Taxis are easy to get when you really don't need them, like getting a bank loan. I carefully checked my RV-8 and its loading, including a test of my oxygen system. I started the engine and taxied a bit to check out every aspect except actual flight. I had to get it right this time. I just could not call home and say I had another delay.

On the entire trip, I had never delayed a departure when it was in my control, not even for weather. Until now. I went over to the FAA flight-service station and asked for a thorough weather briefing. It promised to be good. No bad stuff around and the winds looked okay. At that time of year, the winds were mixed and variable and that was the forecast: generally easterly wind next to the islands, and later, westerly ones. Up around twenty thousand feet and higher, the winds were generally more westerly. That's what I wanted and why I brought oxygen. Dean Stahr, who was flying west, had to wait in California about two weeks for favorable winds to develop. Had I left the States during summer as I originally planned, the winds at twenty thousand feet could have offered me tailwinds of fifty to a hundred knots or more. I would love to have sailed home at three hundred miles an hour. Not this time.

I went around and said good-bye to all those whom I had met at the airport. As a pilot, I find it hard not to meet people at airports, mostly other pilots but they are the best sort. Almost like Will Rogers, I never met a pilot I didn't like.

Watsonville

Honolulu to California was going to be the longest leg of my trip, about twenty-one hundred nautical miles (twenty-four hundred statute miles). I did not bother with dinner and just ate some of my emergency rations: energy bars with water. That's better anyway for the upcoming fourteen-hour sit-down.

I had a terrible time getting the hours to pass until my departure time. I rechecked the weather and found it was the same as before, but the wind speeds had increased a bit. Now it was headwinds of ten to fifteen knots on the early part of the route, and tailwinds of twenty-five to thirty knots for the remainder. That scenario added five or ten tailwind knots. I had already filed my flight plan when I visited the flight-service station, so I called clearance delivery, activated my flight plan and requested permission to taxi for takeoff. As I was cleared, the controller wished me a good flight home, and I was off into the dark skies over Honolulu.

I climbed slowly at two hundred feet per minute, setting a direct heading for the San Francisco Bay area. This was not one of those inky black nights. Stars were out and, at least initially, the lights of Oahu shone brightly. After a while I switched over from VHF to HF, reported in, and then put Beethoven's Ninth on my little portable DVD player. It just doesn't get any better than that. I was going home after over two months on a star-lit night, the music was great, my oxygen system was working normally, and my engine was purring like a kitten. I had filed for twenty-one thousand feet but when I reached seventeen thousand, it was too cold to go higher. I had bought a sweater at a thrift shop in Kailua to replace my high-altitude down jacket, which was destroyed in the fire at Phuket, but it was a lousy substitute. I had on normal underwear, silk long johns, silk *and* regular socks, regular clothes under my flight suit with the sweater over everything, but it wasn't good enough. My airplane had a heater powered by a muff of an exhaust pipe, and it could keep my feet hot while the rest of me froze.

I called Honolulu and amended my flight plan to seventeen thousand, and the controller gave me a block altitude clearance from eleven to seventeen thousand. That indicated what I already suspected—there would be nobody else traveling at those altitudes that day. I made my hourly position reports, first to Honolulu and then later to San Francisco. Flying is one of my passions, and I still get a thrill each and every time I break the surly bonds of earth, but after several hours in the dark with no activity other than position reports and listening to Beethoven, the time started to pass very slowly.

The sun came up sooner than it otherwise might have, since I was fairly high and traveling eastward. At about one thousand miles out of Honolulu, I called Radio San Francisco. On this route, all pilot reports over the ocean go through Radio San Francisco, which is operated by a contractor, but they maintain no records so they have to call the FAA, where all pilot reports are relayed. I wanted an update on the winds aloft for the last half of the leg, and Radio SF said they would get back to me after calling the FAA.

About half an hour later, they called me and said, "The FAA reports that the winds have increased in velocity from twenty-five gusting to thirty-five knots, to thirty-five gusting to forty-five knots at zero four zero." (wind from zero four zero degrees magnetic) My heading was zero four five, so I could expect forty to forty-five knots virtually on the nose. Those are stiff winds and the news made me sit up straight, because the wind direction was diametrically opposite of the forecast.

I knew I had about half the distance to go and about half the fuel on board. An airspeed of one hundred fifty-five knots and headwinds of forty five left me with one hundred ten knots of groundspeed. One thousand miles to go divided by one hundred ten meant about nine hours to fly and I had only six hours' worth of fuel. My sleep-deprived brain couldn't handle more precision than that, so I reached for pen and paper to do a more accurate calculation. Then I remembered I had a marvelous little computer called a global positioning system to do all that work for me.

First I punched in the data necessary for the device to calculate the actual wind speed and direction at my location. It indicated that I still had very mild headwinds, so I decided to continue on the present heading and periodically use the GPS to check the fuel needed to return to Honolulu. The reading was mildly reassuring but it certainly did not eliminate my anxiety. I don't think I was sleepy, despite not having slept for over two days and flying for over six hours, but when you are way out over an ocean in an airplane and get news that there is an unfavorable, seventy-five-knot shift in wind conditions, it produces a supremely heightened state of alertness and a faster heartbeat. I kept track of the wind as I flew on, still uneasy.

After a while, the winds became tailwinds, and still later increased in velocity to coincide with the FAA report, but at two hundred twenty degrees instead of zero four zero, exactly one hundred eighty degrees off the reported direction. I guess that degree of variance was close enough for government work. Then again, maybe I should thank them for keeping me wide awake.

The winds remained favorable all the way to California. According to the calculations done by the GPS, the arrival time I gave my wife now looked right on the money, except for my forgetting about daylight savings time in California. That made me a little giddy in my high state of alertness. A little fiddling with the GPS, listening to Mozart and the airplane and systems working perfectly made the time vanish. About two hundred miles out, I saw the ever-present marine layer of low clouds that marks the northern California coastline in the spring and summer.

After another half-hour or so, I advised Radio San Francisco that I would be leaving HF in order to contact Monterey approach control on VHF and thanked them for their services. I established contact with Monterey approach and, because of the low-lying marine layer, asked for the instrument approach into Watsonville called the localizer two.

Then I realized that the data card I had in the Garmin 430 had only an international database, so the approach procedure into Watsonville wasn't in it. I knew the procedure but couldn't remember the frequency for the localizer. I had the data card containing the information for all the U.S. airports, but I did not want to fiddle around trying to change data cards as I was approaching the airport.

I didn't want to ask the controller for it, as I thought that would be an admission of not having all available information for the flight, a violation of Federal Air Regulations. I guess I was still skittish from being confronted by police so often on the trip and groggy from fatigue, and I didn't want my last act on the last leg to result in a violation. I now realize I could have explained that I simply didn't want to fool around trying to change data cards on approach. Anybody would buy that argument, right? Instead, I just guessed at it.

I knew I had guessed wrong when the controller told me I had flown right through the localizer. "No matter, I think I see a hole over Watsonville so I will cancel IFR at this time," I said. I whizzed over to the break in the clouds and did a quasi-split S down under the layer to land on runway two zero at Watsonville. My speed got a bit high because of my hot dog maneuver and the landing would not have taken a prize.

A follow-me truck appeared in front of me on the taxiway. "Strange," I thought. "Must have something to do with the air show that starts tomorrow." Exiting the taxiway on the ramp, the truck took an unexpected turn to the right and led me right under the largest American flag I had ever seen, hanging from the long ladder of a fire truck.

There was a crowd of people. I thought they had made a mistake and gotten me mixed up with one of the air-show performers. I got the cut-engine signal and then I saw one of my friends run over to my plane with a beer. I greatly appreciated that beer and gradually realized this whole thing was for me. I knew my Shirley would be there to greet me, although I had told her to wait until I called from the airport, but the presence of the other hundred people was a fantastic surprise.

My fellow EAA members had worked up a great homecoming, complete with a party afterward in the EAA hangar. Radio, print, and TV reporters were there, along with my EAA, QB(Quiet Birdmen — an association of experienced pilots), and personal friends, as well as the third-grade class from Gault Elementary School, which had followed my progress around the world as a class geography project. They held up a big banner saying "WELCOME HOME BILL".

I had to look for Shirley, who hung back to allow other people to greet me. That's the way she is. It was great to see her and I was reminded how wonderfully generous she is to support me in the kind of venture I had just completed, and how lucky I am to be married to such a great gal. I was delighted to be home and realized that I had just finished a truly remarkable trip. The flying was challenging but fun. In fact the whole trip was fun, and all the "trouble" added great color to a magnificent adventure. What really made the trip was all the wonderful people I met along the way.

And I have to say I had the support of numerous friends who followed my adventures. I especially need to thank Bob Sliter, EAA webmaster, who was in constant contact with Shirley, comforting her when I could not call, and assisting in the acquisition of spare parts and a hundred other things. And I need to thank all those who took the trouble to come out to the airport to make my return such a memorable event.

I think I have sent e-mails to all those in the U.S. and other countries who befriended me, helped me on my way, or just sent e-mails wishing me well, but I will say it again here: — thank you. Thank you all for your friendship, and for convincing me that, the world conflicts notwithstanding, there are beautiful, friendly people all over the world.

Giant flag courtesy of the Watsonville Fire Dept., arranged by the airport manager. Some welcoming banner.

Shirley and old geezer.

Epilogue

When I returned home I was amazed at the interest my trip generated. More people care about aviation than I could have imagined. I was asked to talk about the adventure by my own and a number of other Chapters of the Experimental Aircraft Association across the state and of course my own Hangar of Quiet Birdmen. (a fraternity of very experienced military, airline and private pilots). I also spoke at several airshows including the largest of all at Oshkosh and several flying clubs including flying doctors. Those are all pilot groups and some interest might be expected. I also talked to a large number of non-aviation groups such as S.I.R.S., rotary, Kiwanis and even a womens club. I estimate that the total population of the combined groups was on the order of twenty five hundred people — amazing and proof that private aviation is not dead. At almost every meeting I was asked if I was going to write a book about my adventure. Writing is not my forte but Shirley's urging finally got me moving.

One can expect to get bills from various countries for "navigation" and other charges after returning home. I received bills from Hadid, the Syrian flight services company who obtained permits for Saudi Arabia, Egypt, Iran, and Pakistan. They were quite efficient and their charges reasonable. I also received several bills from Australia for navigation, special customs services (that official in Broome got back at me), botanical inspection, and fumigation (which I did not have).

I received a bill from International Air Transport Association on behalf of Oman. At first I didn't think I was ever in Omani airspace, but upon reviewing the chart, I found that there is a little triangular projection of Oman's FIR across the air route from Dubai to Karachi. That way they trap every airliner into paying about twelve hundred dollars or more per flight. I was in Omani airspace for about five minutes, and never talked to Omani air traffic control . They billed me six hundred dollars, or about one hundred twenty dollars per minute.

I wrote to IATA and pointed out that the typical airliner weighs about 300,000 pounds, whereas my plane had a MTOW(maximum take off weight) of 2,400 pounds that day, or a ratio of 125 to 1. After several exchanges, they lowered the bill to three hundred dollars, which I paid. Bless you, Oman.

After all that, would I do it again? Absolutely. I did plan another 'round-the-world trip. This time it would be to the north, as I would have gone had I finished building my plane in time. I wanted to go via Goose Bay; Narsasauaq, Greenland; Reyjavik, Iceland; Oslo; Helsinki; St. Petersburg; across Russia and Siberia; to Alaska and southward home, in the summer.

Through an old friend, I had a Russian outfit in Vladivostok estimate the cost for me. I would have had to position fuel across the eastern regions of Russia and Siberia, as avgas is hard to find now in those areas, although jet fuel is readily available. I would still need to find a place to put an auxiliary gas tank other than in the rear cockpit, in order to accommodate a Russian navigator. And I did build an aluminum tank to fit entirely within the aft baggage bay, freeing up the rear cockpit.

When the estimate came back as one hundred seventy thousand dollars just to cross Russia, I scrapped the plan. I later modified the route to go from St. Petersburg via Turkestan to Kunming, China; then around the perimeter of China to Sapporo, Japan; then Kamchatka, Russia; northward and across the Bering Strait to Alaska. This also proved too tough, mainly for bureaucratic reasons—a Chinese sponsor on the ground is required—and lack of avgas. Someday, maybe we will have diesel or turbine engines cheap enough for small aircraft, and then with jet fuel readily available almost everywhere, the traveling will be easier by orders of magnitude. Well, except for the bureaucracy, which grows to offset the effects of any technological advances.

I am certainly not the first to fly either around the world or over the oceans, but the sky is still the same with all its beauty, clouds, fog, and storms, which can and do rip airplanes apart like paper toys. While weather forecasting has improved, the information available to pilots without real-time, world-communications capability is about the same as in the old days. The water below is still the same, with all its expanse and hostility, should one be so unfortunate as to fall within its grasp. The fatigue is the same, and if you run into mechanical trouble, the game is the same: you probably have to be able to fix it yourself. Navigation with GPS is far easier and more certain if all goes well, but the paperwork and bureaucracy are much more difficult and stressful than in the early days. (I think I would trade the uncertainties of navigation for the frustrating bureaucracy.) Still, flying around the world is one of the last great challenges in general aviation. With a diesel engine, I might still be the oldest Earthrounder…someday.

Navigation Documents

Charts

The only charts I took on my flight were IFR enroute charts prepared by the Department of Defense and the Geospatial Intelligence Agency. These are similar to the charts prepared by the FAA.

Terminal Procedures

These are also DOD documents containing:

Radar instrument approach minimums
Standard terminal arrivals
Instrument approach procedures
Airport diagrams

Jeppesen Approach Plates

While the DOD documents contain instrument-approach plates (procedures), I like the Jeppesen documents better so I took approach plates for each of my planned stops.

GPS

The instrument-approach procedures for all airports were contained in the database of my Garmin 430 GNS , and I primarily relied on these.

Form No. 913

GENERAL DECLARATION

I.C.A.O. Annex 9, Appendix 1
(Outward/Inward)

Owner or Operator ...WILLIAM RANDOLPH...

Marks of
Nationality and Registration ...USA...N978DZ...Flight No. PRIVATE Date 18-05-09

Departure from CAIRNS AUSTRALIA... Arrival at LA TONTOUTA NEW CALEDONI

(Place and Country)   (Place and Country)

FLIGHT ROUTING

("Place" Column always to list origin, every en-route stop and destination)

PLACE	(1) TOTAL NUMBER OF CREW	(2) NUMBER OF PASSENGERS ON THIS STAGE	CARGO
CAIRNS	1		
LA TONTOUTA		NONE	
		Departure Place:	
		Embarking........................	
		Through on	NONE
		same flight.......................	Cargo
		Arrival Place:	Manifest Attached
		Disembarking......................	
		Through on	
		same flight.......................	

Declaration of Health

Persons on board known to be suffering from illness other than airsickness or the effects of accidents, as well as those cases of illness disembarked during the flight:

NONE

Any other condition on board which may lead to the Spread of disease:

NONE

Details of each disinsecting or sanitary treatment (place, date, time, method) during the flight. If no disinsecting has been carried out during the flight give details of most recent disinsecting:

NONE

Signed, if required ....
Crew Member Concerned

For official use only

This document required
Upon entry and exit
each country. The only
document consistently
demanded

I declare that all statements and particulars contained in this General Declaration, and in my supplementary forms required to be presented with this General Declaration are complete, exact and true to the best of my knowledge and that all through passengers will continue/have continued on the flight.

SIGNATURE ....
Authorised Agent or Pilot-in-Command

International Flight Plan Form

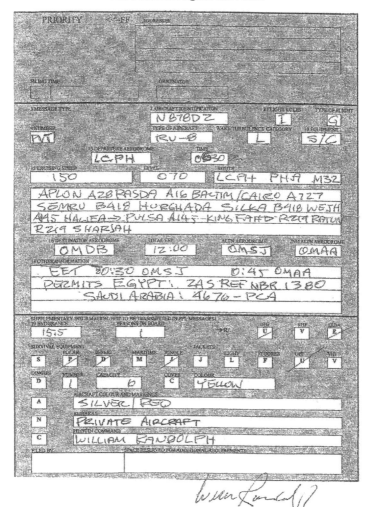

An example of an international flight plan. This one is from
Paphos, Cyprus to Dubai, UAE via Egypt and Saudi Arabia.
Names like APLON are waypoints on the route and A28 is a
designated airway as is A16, A727, etc

International flight plans.

General Requirements For Overseas Flights (In 2005)

Experimental Aircraft

    The RV-8 is an experimental aircraft (not certified by the FAA under ICAO rules). The FAA requires that a written permit from every foreign country be obtained before entry.

High-Frequency Radio

    A long-range (high frequency) radio is required for ocean crossings, and for great landmasses where radar coverage is not available for air-traffic-control purposes. This is not required within the U.S. and it can be quite expensive for an FAA-approved version.

Permits

    Many countries require permits for overflight or landing. Saudi Arabia, Indonesia, and China require a responsible person on the ground within the country to obtain the permit. There may be others as well.

Position Reports

    Over large bodies of water, position reports are required for air-traffic-control purposes. Ocean crossings, in my experience, require position reports every hour. Best to have a GPS to accomplish this. Sextants may serve well for old-fashioned hands but the GPS is dead simple. The reports include latitude and longitude, airspeed, altitude, heading, wind direction, and speed, all of which the GPS can provide.

Routes

Most countries require aircraft to fly only on approved air routes, no direct flights or wandering as in the U.S. The penalties for not doing so range from a tongue-lashing to jail and being shot down.

Documentation

The pilot in command is supposed to carry his personal documentation, such as pilot license, medical certificate, radio station and operators permit, passport, visa (as applicable), vaccination record (some countries), proof of aircraft liability insurance (some countries), aircraft registration, pilots' operating handbook, and weight and balance documents for each flight. In addition, all pilots in command must file a general-declaration document on arrival and departure, and of course a flight plan (ICAO variety). On my trip, no one ever asked for anything other than the general-declaration document, overflight/landing permit, flight plan, visa, and passport.

Equipment

There is no general equipment requirement in the United States, but Transport Canada requires exposure suits and flotation devices when departing Canada over the Northern Atlantic routes. Good sense dictates a long list of survival equipment. Mode S transponders are required in some places above certain altitudes.

Equipment And Operational Data

Aircraft
    Van's Aircraft/Randolph RV-8

Engine
    Lycoming O-360A1A 180 hp

    Avionics
    Garmin 340 Audio/Marker/Intercom System
    Garmin 430 Global Navigation System, which includes:
        Navigation and communication radios,
        Instrument landing system radios and provision for
        databases
        for navigation aids, instrument approach procedures,
        radio
        Frequencies and airports for the entire world
        GPS receiver

    Garmin G106 course deviation indicator
    Garmin SL40 transceiver
    Garmin GTX327 transponder
    Narco 122D navigation and ILS system
    ICOM 706II high frequency transceiver
    Sandia SAE 5-35 altitude data system
    ICOM A-22 handheld navigation and communications
    radio with dry cell battery pack

Garmin 195 handheld GPS with new dry cell battery pack
Waterproof containers for handheld devices such as GPS
and radio transceiver

Headset
Bose Aviation X, active noise-canceling (the RV-8 is noisy)

Autopilot
Trutrak Flight Systems Digitrak w/ altitude hold
coupled to coupled to Garmin 430.

Survival
ACK E-O1 waterproof satellite emergency locator trans-
mitter
TSO'd Part 135 life raft with cover, strobe, desalinization
kit, flares, water, food, signaling mirror, dye markers, and
fishing gear
SOS constant-wear life vest and TSO'd life vest
Knife, extremely sharp for cutting harnesses
Flashlights: two, with extra batteries

Other Equipment
Mountain High oxygen system (21 cu. ft., 55 hours at
15,000 feet)

Special Clothing
Nomex flight suit with pockets for evacuation equipment
Down jacket for cold at high altitude
Silk long johns and socks

Relief
> Travel John (sealable plastic bags with instant gel material), 30 ea.

Travel Rations
> PowerBars and water

Additions and Modifications to Airframe
> Modifications: replaced bolts securing canopy frame to roller track with hitch pins to allow jettisoning canopy before ditching

> Additions:
> Two auxiliary gas tanks—fiberglass/epoxy on ¼-inch foam core
> Tank one—fifteen gallons in forward baggage bay
> Tank two—sixty-eight gallons in aft cockpit and aft baggage bay
> Fuel lines from auxiliaries, each with shutoff valve
> Joining a Flow Ezy fuel filter, then to third port of main fuel selector valve. All gravity fed, no transfer required
> High-frequency antenna—fixed long wire, seven-plus meters
> Nylon line—fifteen feet attached to mid-cockpit frame (bar) and to life-raft-inflation handle

Navigation Information
> International databases for G430 and G195
> DOD terminal information publication, selected volumes including
> instrument-approach procedures and airport diagrams

DOD high and low enroute IFR charts
Jeppesen ILS approach plates for planned stops
ICAO flight plan and general-declaration forms

Aircraft Documentation
Registration
Pilots' operating handbook
Weight and balance calculations at maximum take off weight
Airworthiness certificate
Radio station license
Liability insurance certificate

Money
$30,000 cash in $100 bills
$10,000 travelers checks for use at banks and perhaps hotels
Credit cards for hotels and possibly fuel

OPERATIONAL DATA

General target altitude: 8000 ft.

Hawaii mainland: 21,000 ft. (17,000 actual)

Speed: short legs, under 1000 nautical miles, 180 KTAS (knots true air speed), 75 percent power @ 8000ft
long legs, 155 KTAS, 55 percent

Fuel burn: short legs, 75 percent power, 10 GPH (gallons per hour)
long legs, 55 percent, 7.5 GPH
all rich of peak (carbureted engine)

Maximum still air range at 8000 ft. and 55 percent, 2,500 nautical mi.

    (2,875 statute mi), longer at reduced power

Glossary

Aileron   Hinged flight-control surfaces attached to the
                 trailing edge of the wing, used to control the
                 aircraft in roll.

Airway   A designated route delineated by radio naviga-
                 tion beacons called VOR, for VHF Omnidirec-
                 tional Radio range.

AIS   Aviation Information Services, which include
                 meteorology, flight planning, and other sig-
                 nificant information.

ALTITUDE   An autopilot function used to maintain a set
HOLD   altitude.

ATTITUDE   The inclination of an aircraft relative to the
                 ground

ATC   Air traffic control.

ATIS   Aviation terminal information system, a radio
                 broadcast of information needed for aircraft
                 flight operations at an airport, including al-
                 timeter setting, wind direction and velocity,
                 runway in use, and other pertinent informa-
                 tion such as runway conditions and visibility.

AVIONICS   Radios and other electronic devices (such as
                GPS) for communication, navigation, traffic
                alerts, data gathering, and other specialized
                uses.

CDI   Course deviation indicator, a cockpit
                instrument with needles or bars that show
                when an aircraft is on or off, broadcasts
                radio beams laterally when accompanied
                by a VOR or a localizer receiver, and ver-
                tically when accompanied by a glide-slope
                receiver.

ELEVATOR   A flap-like structure on the tail of an airplane
                to control the aircraft in pitch.

EMPENNAGE   Tail of an airplane.

FIR   Flight information region—airspace with de-
                fined boundaries.

FISHTAIL   Wagging the tail back and forth to cause skid-
                ding and the resulting aerodynamic drag.

GLIDE SLOPE   A fan-shaped, vertical radio beam for vertical
                guidance. One of two radio beams in an ILS.

HF   High frequency—radio operation in a band
                immediately below 30 MHz, used for long-
                range voice communications.

HOLD   Stop and wait at a designated point or maintain a race track pattern at a designated point and altitude.

ILS   Instrument landing system, which has two fan-shaped radio beams, one for horizontal and one for vertical guidance. A cockpit instrument with horizontal and vertical needles or indicators to show the aircraft position relative to each beam centerline. Onboard radio receivers drive each needle.

LOCALIZER   A fan-shaped horizontal radio beam for lateral guidance. Can stand alone or be part of an ILS.

MTOW   Maximum take off weight

NOTAM   Notice to airmen—notification of significant information affecting a planned flight, such as runway closures, out-of-service navigation aids, airspace restrictions, and hazards.

POSITION REPORTS

Reports to ATC of aircraft position at designated reporting points or time intervals. Report consists of, at least, aircraft ID, position, speed, altitude, and heading.

RUDDER   A vertical flap-like structure on the tail to control left and right movements or yaw of an aircraft.

SIGMET   Significant meteorological conditions, such as low visibility, icing, thunderstorms, turbulence, wind shear, freezing rain, etc.

TRANSCEIVER
                A radio capable of both transmitting and receiving.

VHF   Very high frequency—radio operation in the 30–300 MHz band, used for short-range, line-of-sight communications.

VOR   A transmitter emitting a coded signal for each of 360 degrees which can be decoded by a VOR receiver in an aircraft as an aid to navigation.

WING LEVELER
                An autopilot function whose job it is to keep the wings level when engaged.

Made in the USA
Lexington, KY
29 January 2012